# BOUDIC

Boudicca, Queen of the Iceni, was very tall, fearful looking, with a harsh voice and lots of tawny hair which fell to her hips. She was the wife of Prasutagus, King of a British tribe that occupied what is now Norfolk, eastern Cambridgeshire and northern Suffolk, from the 1$^{st}$ Century B.C. until the 1$^{st}$ Century A.D.

The Iceni were friendly towards the Romans and said they respected their army. However, they revolted in A.D. 47, but were deprived of their weapons. Prasutagus died about A.D.60 He had made Roman Emperor, Nero, coheir to his kingdom, together with his two daughters. However, Tacitus, a senator of the Roman Empire, relates that the estates of Prasutagus were plundered. Boudicca was flogged and her daughters raped.

The Iceni fought back, ransacking ﹐ Camurlodunum (Colchester), Londinium (London), and Verulamium (St. Albans) and about 70,000 people were killed. The tribes were finally routed but Boudicca slipped away but died in A.D.61 by poison or illness. Boudicca almost ended Roman Rule in Britain.

# ALAN HUGHES

Alan Hughes was born in Upminster, Essex, but moved to Hickling, Norfolk in 1957 when he was 14. His father worked as a bricklayer, but then decided to take the White Horse Pub, in White Horse Common.

Alan got a lot of tools and got a job with Porter and Haylett in Wroxham. He then took a position with Broads Tours and drove a 38ft boat. Then he progressed to a 52ft boat called Princess Pat. While working he found a woman in the water and saved her. He also rescued a young man.

Alan met a girl frm North Walsham called Joan, who he courted and they married in 1964. They had three daughters, Angela, Sandra, and Jane.

Alan moved to Westwick and worked for Ross Foods. He stayed there for 13 years. They moved to North Walsham in 1972 and Alan has lived there ever since.

Alan and Joan got divorced and he was better off as a result. He could deal with his own money and not rely on Joan. He treats his daughters and grand children very generously.

# BLICKLING HALL

Going back a long way, Blickling Manor was owned by King Harold, but after his death at the Battle of Hastings, William the Conqueror, William I bestowed it on Bishop William of Thetford.

Sir Thomas Boleyn owned the Manor, he was the father of Anne Boleyn, a wife of Henry VIII. The last Boleyn owner was Sir James, a brother of Anne and the Manor then passed to the Clere family. Sir Edward Clere lost the family fortune and had to vacate the Manor. Henry Hobart became the tenant but the Manor was in a poor state, he knocked it down and commissioned Robert Lyminge to build a better place – Blickling Hall

Hobart built Blickling Hall with the backing of Sir Francis Bacon. Bacon was a brilliant lawyer. He had a "brainwave" that promoted Edward Coke to Lord Chief Justice of the Kings Bench. Secondly, Sir Henry Hobart should be Lord Chief Justice of the Common Please – leaving the post of Attorney General for Bacon himself.

Sir John Hobart married Frances, and Frances' former friend, Prince Charles, now King Charles I, was three years into his reign. John and Frances were a good living couple and the house was always full of family and friends.

Nowadays, like with so many grand houses, Blickling Hall is administered by the National Trust, as is Felbrigg Hall.

## C.T. BAKER LTD

The business began sometime between 1730 and 1760. It was the Custance family and Adam Custance describes himself as a joiner in Bodham and refers to Ironmongery & Hardware, probably a shop and probably in the nearest town, Holt.

John Baker took over the business and had a son John Baker (junior) in 1775. John Baker junior died in 1867 leaving the business to his two sons, John Sales Baker and Charles Baker.

It seems that Charles Baker carried on the business and his son Charles Thomas Baker (1842-1900) is the C.T. Baker we know the company by to this day.

He only lived until he was 58 but he expanded the business and had branches in Sheringham and Fakenham, and a workforce of 37

On the death of C.T. Baker in 1900, Charles Morton Baker became Chairman, with Mr. J.R. Scoley as Managing director.

By the time war broke out in 1914, all the directors of the company were female, Ros Baker being Chairman. Ros lived in Tunbridge Wells (Kent) and visited Holt once or twice a year.    Directors meetings were held in London.

The period from 1925 – 1939 was relatively uneventful. In the heating department Bakers supplied Aga cookers. In 1939 an agreement was signed giving the company sole distribution rights within a 25 mile radius of Holt.

As Ros was unable to attend meetings she was asked to leave the Board and she sold her shares – 250 to Tom, 300 to Jim, 50 to Jack, 700 to Mary and 701 to Nellie. Ros had stayed with Jim on her visits to Holt but this arrangement stopped and there was virtually no contact between them.

From 1943 to 1950 steady progress was made and dividends were paid as follows – 1943 – 15%, 1944 – 15%, 1945 -15%, 1946 – 20%, 1947 – 20%, 1948 – 20%, 1949 – 20%

Wilfred (Nellie's Husband) died in 1950 and Nellie died in 1955.   Control was in the hands of three brothers. T.H.M. Baker (Tom),  H.J.M. Baker (Jim), C.J.M. Baker (Jacko)  Jim had been in the comapny for 30 years and resented interference from his brothers.

In 1973 the younger members of the family were taking an interest and while Anthony and Miles would not work for the company directly, it was decided that Michael would. In 1974 Michael became director.

From 1973 – 2010 turnover has increassed from £180,000 in 1973 to a figure of eight digits in 2009-2010. Anthony does not agree with Michael's U.K.I.P. politics. Mike drives a van with U.K.I.P. all over it. Anthony feels that Norman Lamb is a good M.P. If you have a problem and you ask for Norman's help, he will try to help, he doesn't know whether you voted Liberal Democrat, Conservative, Labour or U.K.I.P. in 2010

Several important members of staff and the board are due to retire and Mike is likely to retire within five years – he is 69. The new board members will have to be appointed carefully to ensure the progress of the company continuing.

# H. RIDER HAGGARD

William Haggard the owner of Brackham Hall, took his family abroad for the winter. Mrs. Haggard was expecting a baby, so they returned early in May. The Hall had been let for the Winter and was not ready for them to move back in, so she decided to stay at Wood Farm. It was a pleasant thatched house. There, on the 22$^{nd}$ June, 1856, William Haggard's sixth son, Henry Rider Haggard – to be knowns as H. Rider Haggard was born.

As a baby he developed jaundice and the clergyman was hastily summoned and christened him "Henry Rider" on September 22$^{nd}$ 1856

Ella Haggard, H. Rider's mother had only two more children, Mary, born in June 1858 – and Arthur, who was born just seventeen months after his sister. This completed the family of seven sons and three daughters.

Ten children were not unusual in the nineteenth century. Remember, Queen Victoria had nine.

Once Rider thought he heard the swish of a silk skirt in his room. The old tale of how Lady Hamilton, when she came to stay at Bradenham with Nelson's sister, Mrs.

Bolton, slept in the East Room, of the stiff silks she loved to wear and which hung in the big wardrobe in the corner, came back to his mind. He pulled the clothes over his head, and fell into an uneasy doze in which he dreamt he was a rat being chased by an enormous ferret in a tunnel, which got narrower and narrower. Suddenly he woke up.

When he was thirteen Rider was sent to Rev. Mr. Graham of Garsington Rectory, near Oxford. Rider loved the land and was happiest in the dairy or riding home on the last loads at harvest.

Rider was sent to Ipswich Grammar School, later to a private tutor in London and then to the crammer schools, to be coached for the Foreighn Office Entrance Examination.

One night, at a dance in Richmond, Rider fell headlong in love. Sir Henry Bulwer, of Heydon, in Norfolk, was going out as Lieutenant-Governor of Natal. William Haggard thought Rider could go with him, Sir Henry agreed. So at nineteen, Rider Haggard was sent to Africa.

Rider fell in love with Africa, he wrote four books – "Nada the Lily", "Marie", "Child of Storm" and "Finished", about the Zulus.

Rider also loved Madiera and wrote "Dawn" about the island.

**Two hearts that beat as one**

The first two signatures to a letter calling for funds to finance "The Liberty League" are those of Sir Rider Haggard and Mr. Rudyard Kipling.

"Every Bolshi is a blackguard" said Kipling to Haggard

"And given to tippling" said Haggard to Kipling

"And a blooming outsider" said Rudyard to Rider
"Their domain is a blood yard" said Rider to Rudyard

"That's just what I say" said the author of They
"I agree, I agree" said the author of She

H. Rider Haggard's major works were "King Solomon's Mines" and "She". He died in 1925

# HOUGHTON HALL

Houghton Hall was begun in 1722 for Sir Robert Walpole, generally regarded as Brittain's first Prime Minister. He was Prime Minister to George I and George II.

The building material was a locally sourced farm coloured brick. Houghton Hall is a little before Holkham Hall but they are both magnificent Palladian houses.

The Hall was designed to house Walpole's prized collection of Old Master Paintings. There is a superb interior and furnishings designed by William Kent. The paintings still hang in their original positions.

The medieval St. Martin's Church sits within the deer park, where there is a herd of fallow deer and smaller groups of more exotic species. There are over 150 varieties in the rose garden, also a kitchen garden, glass houses, sculptures and the fountain "Waterflame" by Jeppe Hein.

The owner now is a direct descendant of Sir Robert Walpole – the 7th Marquess of Cholmondeley (Pronounced Chumley).

Houghton Hall is just off the A148 between King's Lynn and Fakenham.

## NORMAN LAMB M.P.

Herbert Lamb, Norman's father, was Professor of Climatology at the University of East Anglia in Norwich. Moira Lamb, Norman's mother, lives in Holt and is President of North Norfolk Liberal Democrats.

Norman was educated at Wymondham College and then went on to Leicester University where he did a law degree – L.L.B. He became a solicitor before deciding he would like a career in politics. He was selected as Liberal Democrat Candidate for North Norfolk in 1990 and lost the election in 1992 to Sir Ralph Howell. Sir Ralph retired and in 1997 Norman took on David Prior and lost again. However, in 2001, Norman defeated David Prior by a small majority (483)

In 2005 the Conservatives selected Iain Dale to stand against Norman, but Norman won with a majority of merely 11,000.

Mike Baker, of C.T. Baker Ltd., stood for U.K.I.P. He drives a van with U.K.I.P. advertised all over it. His cousin Anthony Baker doesn't agree with Mike and asked him if he intended to visit, not to use the van.

Norman Lamb, M.P., doesn't advertise so obviously. He just tries to help anybody in North Norfolk, who has a problem, whether they voted Liberal Democrat, Conservative, Liberal or U.K.I.P.

Norman was a Government Whip and in February 2012 was placed in the Business Department. He became Care Minister in September 2012. Norman will stand for election again in 2015. He must feel he still has a lot more to do.

Norman is married to Mary and they have two sons, Archie and Ned.

Simon Wright was Norman's agent in 2005 and in 2010 stood and won Norwich South from Charles Clarke. When Norman heard the news at the count in Cromer, he drove to Norwich to congratulate Simon. The only thing Norman had against Simon winning was the fact that he might have to share the media time!!

# STUART EUSTACE

Stuart's father, Ralph Eustace, was born in Penn in Buckinghamshire but moved to Sheringham. He was apprenticed to Saddlers Garage but in 1936 he became an A.A. man on a bicycle. Also in 1936 he married Ivy Smith and they lived at West Lodge, Sheringham. They later moved to North Walsham.

In 1939 Ralph left the A.A. to join the R.A.F. at the start of the Second World War. In 1945 he left the R.A.F. and returned to the A.A. – on a motorcycle and later in a van.

Ralph and Ivy had a son, Stuart in 1948. Ralph got the Queen's Jubilee Medal for service to the community.

Stuart attended the new Millfield School from the age of 5 till 8 and then North Walsham Primary School from 8 to 11. Then he went to North Walsham Secondary Modern School until he left at the age of 15

He became an apprentice at Gleave and Key in White Horse Common, and then worked in sales of cars and machinery and ended up as Service Manager. He then went to the Mundesley Garage, which did Volvos, as Service Manager and later to Hannants until they closed down.

Stuart then joined the Norfolk and Waveney Health Service – drove the mini-bus to the "Heron" coach. He then drove the "Heron" coach for about 10 years. The "Heron" coach was stopped due to cut-backs and Stuart then became a support worker in the community.

While working on the "Heron" coach Stuart also worked in the evenings for the Bure Centre doing "needle" exchange in Cromer, Dereham and Norwich.

Stuart had difficulty in walking and had to have a hip replaced. This was done and then he retired to live in East Ruston.

# TERRY ALCOCK

There was a footballer called Terry
Who, at the beautiful game, could make merry.
He could score with his head,
And both feet, it is said.
As the ball, in the net, he would bury

Terry Allcock was born in Leeds. He attended St. Anthony's Primary School, then St. Joseph's College, but after six months there moved to Mount St. Mary's School

He was captain of Leeds Boys Football Team
He was captain of Yorkshire Boys Football Team
He was captain of North of England & South of England

He played for England v The Rest, with the late great Duncan Edwards.

He played cricket for Yorkshire Boys with Ken Taylor. He opened the batting and kept wicket.

From school he went to play for Bolton Wanderers but was also an apprentice coachbuilder in Blackpool. He made his debut for Bolton at the age of 17 against Manchester City and scored two goals in the first twenty minutes.

Terry did National Service and was Captain of the R.A.F. football team.

At Bolton he played with the legendary Nat Lofthouse. He stayed with Bolton for eight years, from 1950 – 1958, when he signed for Norwich City.

Terry is sometimes regarded as a striker but he regards himself as an inside forward. For seven years he played in midfield but having broken both legs and having various other injuries, he played in defence for five years with Barry Butler, Freddie Sharpe, David Stringer and Laurie Brown.

He finished his playing career in 1970, he had served Norwich City for 12 years. He then had four years as First Team Coach and Youth Team Manager

In 1974 he became coach of Manchester City but soon returned to Norfolk where his family was growing up. He had married Barbara in 1956 and they had four boys and a girl.

Terry part owned a garage in Gt. Yarmouth for 17 years until 1991

He was Captain and Chairman of Sprowston Park Golf Club. Footballers were not that well paid in those days and they needed a summer job. Terry was an M.C.C.

qualified Cricket Coach and Coached at Greshams School, Holt for 10 years – he also played cricket for Norfolk.

Terry scored 127 goals for Norwich City – second only to Johnny Gavin. He was the top goal scorer four years running from 1961-1965. He scored five hat-tricks including a hat-trick of headers. Only Dennis Law and Terry have done that. He scored a hat-trick at Anfield.

Terry was Daily Mirror player of the week when in the first game of the season he netted a hat-trick against Bury. He was Player of the Month when Norwich beat Man. Utd. At Old Trafford in 1966 and he was the first to receive the Barry Butler Trophy for Player of the Year.

He scored seven goals in a week including four against Newcastle in the Cup.

In his most prolific season Terry scored 37 goals – this is still a record.

Paul, Terry's youngest son, was manager of Peter Taylor's Funeral Directors at the age of 21. Taylors sold out to an American company and Paul was not happy. Terry had sold his share in the garage. So in 1999 Paul and Terry started Allcock's Funeral Services in City Road, Norwich. Terry was already 63 years old and agreed to do the driving of the hearse. Paul is now Chairman of Norfolk Undertakers.

There are Paul, Philip, Sharon, Mark and Paul's wife Alison and a grandson and a grandaughter in the business. It is a true "family firm"

Terry is 78 now but still enjoys a round of golf and a game of bowls. He is also host to the Match Sponsors at Carrow Road when Norwich City play at home.

# THE CUBITTS OF BLAKENEY

Charlie Cubitt was born in 1903. He married Annie Wordingham who was a Blakeney girl born in 1916. Charlie was an agricultural engineer at Blakeney Engineering.

They had two daughters, Joyce and Kathy. Joyce went to Wells Secondary Modern School and left at the age of 15. She then worked in Wells and went to work on a small motorcycle. Joyce is married to Dave Waller.

Kathy passed the 11 plus and went to Fakenham Grammar School. She worked for Norwich Union in Upper King Street. She had an interest in horses and although the money was not so good, she worked for Sandon Saddlery in Holt. She had saved some money and has some horses in Wiveton where she bought a house.

Kathy travelled a lot and met her future husband Brian Antuar in Australia. They returned to live in Holt and later moved to High Kelling, a pleasant village just outside Holt. Brian is a Morris Dancer.

## THE FARMING MACKS OF NORFOLK

Richard Mack sen. Farmed at Hole Farm, Hampstead, near Holt. He had five children. Kate, who never married, Eleanor, who didn't marry either, twins Richard and Robert, who died of flu while farming a Calthorpe, and George.

After leaving Hempstead, Richard's son farmed at Baconsthorpe Hall, now in ruins – then he went to Plumstead Hall and his son Richard Jun. Married Gladys Everitt and his children were Ted who was 10, Henry 9, Bob 7, and Janet 2½.

Ted was born at Mount Farm, Edgefield in 1916, went to live with his grandparents in Banningham and then Thurgarton Hall, later Row Hall, Wood Norton. Ted began farming at Grove Farm, Heydon and Janet worked for Ted during the Second World War. Ted reared a pedigree herd of Friesians. He married Maisee Mandford and had three children, Ann, Susan and John. He sold his herd of cows and bought Pond Farm, Bodham and his son John, farms there now. Ann is now Mrs. John Lockhart and Susan is Mrs. Ian Stiff.

Henry came to Hempstead Hall from Plumstead Hall at the age of 15. He took over the farm and farmed there until he retired and his son William took over. Henry was a Churchwarden for 51 years. Henry died in 2009 aged 91

Bob was in the Territorial Army and was called up in 1939 for the Royal Norfolk Regiment. He served in India and France. On his return to England he transferred to the Royal Engineers, serving in North Africa and Italy where he was demobbed in 1946. He married Pat in 1947. They had three children, Richard, born in 1948, Aileen born in 1950 and Steven born in 1956.

Bob and Pat Wed at Court Green, Hempstead. Pat was a teacher at Langham Primary School. Richard is an agricultural engineer in Spooner Row. Aileen worked as a nursery nurse and has returned to Norfolk to live in Mindesley. Stephen is a fertilizer consultant for Barnhams of Fakenham.

William is a working farmer. He used to play cricket for Holt and enjoys a game of snooker. His wife, Lynda, runs the Bed and Breakfast side of the business at Hempstead Hall.

During the war the biggest bomb crater in Norfolk was created on Hempstead Hall land. It is still called the "bomb" field.

William and Lynda have two children. A son Charles, who lives on the farm and is an agricultural business consultant for Brown and Co. in their Norwich office. Their daughter Lucy is a teacher in Lincolnshire.

Joy Mack was born in 1935. She married John Morter and they live in Morley St. Peter, near Wymondham. They have two children, Philip andChristopher.

Janet enjoys her holidays in Scotland and Wales. She likes a flutter and a smoke.

# THE LAWRENCES

Walter Lawrence lived in Skeyton and worked for F. Randell & Co. Ltd., Agricultural Engineers (The Foundry) in North Walsham where Sainsburys is now. He biked early on and then learned to drive and bought his own car.

He volunterred for the Army and the Royal Navy at the outbreak of World War Two, but because he was in a reserved occupation – helping to make agricultural implements for use on the land for food production – he stayed with Randells. The implements were isssued by the "Ladies Land Army"

He worked at the Foundry for 50 years, after 25 years he received a gold watch and after 50 years he received a television, for loyal service.

He had a large family, four boys and three girls. John Lawrence is the eldest of the seven children. He was born in Skeyton and educated at Skeyton Primary School and North Walsham Secondary Modern. He left at 15 and worked at Bridge Garage, Banningham. He left there at the age of 25 and went to work at Crane's Garage in Marsham. He met Christine Stearman from Marsham, who worked as an egg packer for Norfolk Newlay in Marsham. They were married in 1976.

After 10 years at Cranes, he opened his own Motor Repair Shop in Spa Common and has been working there ever since. He is a member of a Vintage Tractor Club and enjoys gardening and smokes a pipe.

John and Christine have two children, Ann and Peter. There are three grand children

# THE NEWMANS OF FLEGGBURGH (NR. YARMOUTH)

William John Newman was born in Fleggburgh in 1905. He married a local girl, Betty Curtis, the daughter of John Curtis of Fleggburgh, a farmer.

John Curtis had twelve children who had an average of six children each.

Dick Norman, William's son was born on "D-Day" 6th June, 1944. He went to Fleggburgh C of E Primary School and then on to the Technical High School in Gorleston.

When he left school Dick took a job as a junior clerk in a Builders Merchant. He did this for five to six years but Dick had ambitions to be a rep. He went on the road two days a week for Garson Blake and Sons. There was a vacancy for a rep. at Precasters. Dick got it and did it for two years. He was covering Norfolk and parts of Suffolk. His figures were not good and there was a disagreement. Dick left the company and was out of work for a month.

Dick started again as a junior clerk for Malletts of King's Lynn in their Acle depot. He worked his way up to Office Manager and then Manager in Charge of the Depots at Acle and Yarmouth. He left them after a while and decided to work for himself as a gas supplier for a caravan park. He bought a few caravans and rented them out. He had twelve caravans at one point and asked a local farmer to hire some land to put the caravans on. Later he sold the business.

Dick married Jean on 6th June 1964, his twentieth birthday.

Dick and Jean started doing car boots in 1984. They make a small profit which suppliments their Pension.

Away from work Dick was Secretary of the Men's Club, Secretary of the School Parents Association. A parish councellor for a time, secretary to Poor Trustees and later a Poor Trustee himself.

Dick Norman and Jean have three children, Gail, Lynn and Richard.

## THE RT. HON BARONESS SHEPHARD OF NORTHWOLD J.P. D.L.

Gillian Shephard was brought up in Knapton and was Head Girl at North Walsham High School. She went on to Oxford University and obtained an M.A. in Modern Languages.

On leaving university she became a teacher but soon moved on to become a careers adviser and a Primary School Adviser, including teacher training for Primary French, Nuffield Maths etc. She was a Schools Inspector and Senior Education Officer in charge of planning.

Gillian married Thomas Shephard, retired headmaster, who already had two sons.

She was an Administrator and Researcher in Commercial Television.

Gillian was a County Councillor, a Magistrate, a Chairman of West Norfolk and Wisbech Health Authority, then of the Norwich Health Authority. Also she was a Mental Health Act Commissioner and a Lecturer, on the Cambridge Extra Moral Board and the Workers' Educational Association.

In 1987 Gillian Shephard became Conservative M.P. for South West Norfolk, a seat she held untill 1997. She held several posts in Government including Minister of State at H.M. Treasury responsible for indirect taxation – she reformed car taxation in the Budgets of 1991 and 1992.

From 1991-1993 Gillian was Secretary of State for Employment and Minister with Responsibilities for Women. She became Minister of Agriculture, Fisheries and Food from 1993-1994. She moved to become Minister of Education from 1994-1995. In 1995 she added Employment to her responsibilities and set up the Dearing Review of Higher Education. She also introduced literacy and numeracy hours in shools.

From 1997-1998 Gillian was Shadow Leader of the House of Commons. Transferred to become Shadow Secretary of state for Environment, Transport and the Regions. From 2001-2003 Gillian was a Member of the House of Commons select committee on Environment, Food and Rural Affairs.

Gillian Shephard was appointed a Privy Counsellor in 1992. She was a member and worker for so many organisations. At present she is Chairman of the Institue of Education. Chairman of Oxford University Society and a Member of the Royal Society Vision for Science and Mathematices Education 5-19 committee. She was created a Life Baroness in 2005.

She is Chairman of the East of England Bio-Fuels Forum and President of the Video Standards Council.

## THE VAUGHANS OF NORTH NORFOLK

Granville Vaughan was born in Tunstead, Nr. Wroxham. He was a farm worker, but these were poorly paid in those days. He later became a postman in Swanton Abbot and North Walsham. He then worked for Ross Foods until he retired.

His son Malcolm Vaughan was born in 1952 in Swanton Abbot. He attended Swanton Abbot primary school and at the age of 11 he went to North Walsham Secondary Modern School, which he left at the age of 15.

He worked in Swanton Abbot Garage for about two years and then went to work as a Groundsman for North Walsham Education Committee. Then he went into the building trade with William Bird and Son.

He married Jenny in December 2003 at the same chapel in Swanton Abbot that his mother had got married in.

Malcom has stayed in the building trade and is a member of Swanton Abbot Parish Council.

# CECILIA LUCY BRIGHTWELL

Cecilia Lucy Brightwell studied etching under John Sell Cotman and copied etchings of old masters, including Rembrandt and Dumar. She was born in Thorpe St Andrew, Norwich, on 27th February 1811 to Thomas and Mary Brightwell. She is known to have produced at least thirty-five etchings. The majority of her etchings and thirty-two of the copper plates are in Norwich Castle Museum and Art Gallery. She also produced landscape compositions from nature.

Lucy produced illustrations for her father's 1848 book, "Sketch of a Fauna Infusoria for East Norfolk". She was a deeply religious woman and wrote about pious and moral subjects and she was concerned about the mental improvement of the young. She produced more than twenty literary works between 1854-1857. Her most important work being the "Memorials of the Life of Amelia Opie, Selected and Arranged from her Letters and Diaries and other Manuscripts" (1854). Mrs Opie was a family friend and Thomas Brightwell acted as her executor.

Thomas died in 1868 and Lucy wrote 'out of the abundance of the heart' "Memorials of the Life of Mr Brightwell of Norwich" (1869).

In 1864, Lucy suffered the first signs of cataracts, which led to her blindness. In 1874, Lucy was "Attacked by disease of the brain", and died after eight months of severe suffering. She died on the 17th April 1875 at her home in Surrey Street and was buried on the 22<sup>nd</sup> April at the Rosary Cemetary, Norwich.

# EDITH CAVELL

Edith Cavell was one of the bravest women on the planet at the start of the First World War.

Edith Louisa Cavell was born on the 4th December 1865, in Swardeston, near Norwich. She was the first child of the Rev. Frederick Cavell, C of E and his wife Sophia.

Edith was educated at home and then at boarding school. On leaving she became a governess in Brussels, Belgium, where she stayed for six years.

Her father became ill and Edith came back to England in 1895 to help nurse him. She decided to be a nurse and on 3rd September 1896 she enrolled at the London Hospital School of Nursing. She continued her training in Bow and worked at several London hospitals and also in Manchester.

Then she took up a position as director of a nurses training school, the Berkendael Institute in 1907 in Brussels. The school was a new idea in Belgium.

Plans were drawn up for a new building, however, the First World War began, and the plans had to be put on hold. The work of the hospital carried on and Edith began to assist in the escape of allied soldiers. The soldiers were provided with money and guides and were often disguised as patients.

The Germans became suspicious after Edith had helped about 200 prisoners to escape. Edith was arrested on 5th

August 1915 and on 7th August 1915 she was put in solitary confinement.

Nine people were court-martialled on 7th October 1915. Pleas of clemency were heard but Cavell and Baucq were condemned to be shot at dawn on 12th October 1915.

Edith was resigned to her fate and prayed and read. She also wrote letters to her family and friends. There was a lot of diplomatic activity across Europe. The Americans made the biggest effort to save her, but to no avail.

After the war there was a funeral service at Westminster Abbey and on the 15th May1919, she was buried in Norwich Cathedral.

A statue was erected in Edith Cavell's honour at Tombland, Norwich.

# ELIZABETH FRY

Elizabeth Fry (nee Gurney) was born on 21$^{st}$ May 1780, in Magdelyn Street, Norwich. She was the daughter of John and Catherine Gurney, who were Quakers. Her family was quite well known, they included the brothers Joseph John Gurney and Samuel Gurney, who were philanthropists, the banker and antiquery Daniel gurney and Louisa Gurney Hoare. Catherine Gurney died young leaving the younger children to be brought up by the eldest daughter Kitty. Their upbringing was unusual at that time.

When Elizabeth was eighteen years old she reaffirmed her religious beliefs, after hearing the American Quaker, William Savery, speak. Her cousin Priscilla Hannah Gurney and Deborah Darby also inspired her and when she was nineteen she adopted Quaker dress and speech.

On the19th August 1800, Elizabeth Gurney married Joseph Fry (1777-1861), from another Quaker family, which was quite wealthy. The couple had eleven children. They lived at St Mildreds' Court in London and then at Plashet House in East Ham. Elizabeth helped the needy and gave out clothing, food and medicine. She encouraged vaccination and helped to almost eliminate smallpox. In 1811 she was acknowledged as a Quaker   minister.

Elizabeth wanted to improve living conditions for women in prison. She visited Newgate prison in 1813 and was not happy about the overcrowding.

In Norfolk she had led Sunday School. In East Ham she was co-founder of a girls school She introduced many changes to Newgate prison – Prison dress, constant supervision by a matron, and monitors, religious and elementary education, and paid employment. This improved the attitude and conduct of the prisoners. Elizabeth or one of her team would visit Newgate every day. She herself read to the prisoners from the Bible, on Fridays.

In April 1817, the "Ladies' Association for the Reformation of Female Prisoners" was created. This was extended in 1821 into the "British Ladies' Society for promoting the Reformation of Female Prisoners" with correspondents in Russia, Italy, Switzerland and the Netherlands.

Elizabeth then made several journeys through England, Scotland and Ireland, practising her beliefs. She visited prisons, and suggested ways they could be improved. She also helped establish committees for visiting female prisoners. In 1827 she published a handbook "Observations on the Visiting, Superintendence, and Government of Female Prisoners" She followed this in 1840 on "Hints on the Advantages and the Duties of Ladies' Committees who Visit Prisons".

Elizabeth was confronted with opposition to her prison work. However, she persevered, expanding her journeys promoting prison reform, the abolition of slavery and religious tolerance alongside preaching. She established a Maternal Society in Brighton in 1813, libraries for the coastguard of England, several district visiting societies, a servants society and a "Society of Nursing Sisters", the first attempt to reform nursing in Britain.

Elizabeth Fry died on 13th October 1845 in Ramsgate, and was buried in the Quaker burial ground in Barking, Essex, on 20th October.

Elizabeth is commemorated in many places. Two plaques in Norwich, one at Gurney Court, off Magdalen Street, and one at Earlham Hall. At the University of East Anglia, the School of Social Work and Psychology is housed in the Elizabeth Fry building. There is a plaque at St Mildreds' Court, in London, where she lived when she was first married. A bust of Elizabeth adorns the gatehouse of H.M. Prison Wormwood Scrubs. There is a stone statue of her in the Old Bailey. There is also a plaque at Arklow House, where she lived in Ramsgate.

Elizabeth Fry is also depicted on two panels of Quaker Tapestry, panels E5 and E6, and there is an Elizabeth Fry ward at Scarborough Hospital in North Yorkshire.

In May 2002, Elizabeth became only the second woman to appear on a Bank of England note (£5). The first one was Florence Nightingale.

# ANNA SEWELL

Anna Sewell (1820-1878) from Gt. Yarmouth, wrote only one book, "Black Beauty". She was the daughter of Quaker parents and her mother, Mary Sewell, was also a writer.

As a girl, Anna showed an interest in natural history and was a good drawer. Anna liked horses     and learnt to ride and drive. She never married and lived with her parents.

"Black Beauty" was written between 1871-1877, when Anna's health was poor and she was confined  to the home on her sofa.

The book was published in November 1877 and has become a children's classic. Anna died just five months after the publication, so she saw the start of its success.

# "YODELLING" REGGIE FULLER

On the evenings of 14th, 15th and 16th October 1937, the queues at the Regal Cinema, Holt were larger than normal. At the last performance on Saturday night people had to be turned away. The film showing was Ralph Lynn and Tom Walls in "For Valour" billed as comrades in battle, partners in crime. It wasn't just the film people wanted to see – live on stage during the interval was 15 year old "Yodelling" Reggie Fuller billed as Holt's wonder boy. He had recently left school and was working as a projectionist in the cinema at Sheringham.

He appeared on stage, a tiny figure in a blue blazer and white flannels. Showing no signs of nervousness, he started off with "I have a Swiss Miss" – a yodelling song he had learned from a gramophone record belonging to his grandmother – ending his act by leading the audience in popular songs on his harmonica. At the conclusion, after taking two bows, the Regal manager, Mr. S.G. Oliver announced that Reggie was waiting to go to London to appear at the B.B.C. He said that the directors of East Coast Cinemas wished him all the best and they might one day see Reggie Fuller's name appear in lights. Mr. H.W. Moulton was then introduced to present Reggie with a Minevitch professional harmonica on behalf of East Coast Cinemas. He said "Reggie is helping put Holt on the map and as a businessman I appreciate this."He wished him all the best and was certain he would go far.

It wasn't generally known but earlier that year before the cinema had opened, he had tried the effect of yodelling in an empty hall- never to imagine that that before the year was out he would be standing in the spotlight on the stage. The result of all this was due to an audition he had attended in February at the Regal Theatre, Gt. Yarmouth. All that week Carrol Levis the Canadian Bandleader was holding auditions for his "Discovery Show", which was broadcast on Radio Luxemburg. Reggie arrived with his parents just as the auditions were closing on the Friday. After his father Mr Archie Fuller had explained they had just travelled forty miles (quite a journey in those days) Mr Levis decided to hear him. "Where is your music?" called Mr Levis' voice from the darkness. "Here it is" said Reggie, producing a small harmonica from out of his pocket. "All right then shoot" said Mr Levis and Reggie obliged. He was so successful he was asked to appear in the show that night and again on Saturday.

On the Sunday night of 16<sup>th</sup> March 1937 at 10.30pm, Reggie was heard by Holt, and the nation, on Radio Luxemburg receiving a great number of votes from the listeners and proving to be one of Carrol Levis most popular discoveries. He went on to win the Great Britain Talent Contest at the Odeon, Leicester Square. The Bandleader was so impressed with young Reggie he wanted him to go on tour with him but Mr Fuller was reluctant to let him go due to his age and the current situation in Europe. It's ironic that within a few years, he was called up and left home anyway.

Before joining the RAF in 1942 he ran and worked as the projectionist in the cinema on Weybourne Camp, inspiring his younger brother Archie Jr to later take up the same profession at Holt. After training at Blackpool he was stationed at Wittering. It was there he took part in many entertainment shows playing many roles including Pantomime, representing the RAF and also appearing on the radio programme called "Aircraftsman Smith Entertains".

He met his future wife Denise in 1945 when he was stationed near Luton and it wasn't until six months later she learned about his famous past from his parents. After demob Reggie stayed in Luton and along with a partner called Ken Moody, became entertainers called "The Bunkhouse Boys". He was the "Yodelling Cowboy" playing the ukulele whilst Ken played the accordion.

He married Denise in 1949 and moved to St Albans, still entertaining whenever possible and often appearing on the radio with Cyril Levis (Carrol's brother)

In 1968 he became involved with the "Independent Order of Foresters" and helped to form a caravan group, which really took off. He went to Canada with them in 1982, his voice and ukulele working overtime. He performed at every stop and was well received.

Moving back to Luton in 1986 he would often be called upon to sing on many occasions, regularly entertaining his friends and their children as "Davey Crockett", with Denise dressed as his squaw.

They decided to move to Norfolk in March 1996, buying a chalet bungalow in North Walsham. Sadly he had a heart attack in the June and passed away after only three months of moving. People who knew him said he was always a very modest man and did not realise that had he continued this as his career he could have become famous. If his father, Mr Fuller, had decided to let him tour with Carrol Levis would "Yodelling" Reggie Fuller have been a household name, would we have seen his name in lights as Mr Oliver had announced that night at the Regal and would he have made any recordings for all to enjoy? Who knows?

Thinking of the limited amplication in the 1930's, that small lad must have had an incredible voice to project it in some of those large halls.

# FREDA STARR AND CLEY

Freda Starr was born in 1904 in Lakenheath, Suffolk but her family moved to Cley in 1906, when she was two.

Her father took over a general stores, which he ran until ill health forced him to retire in 1937. Freda and her sister took over, with the help of Charlie Francis. Freda was the proprietor until 1973, when she was 69. She never married, dedicating her life to the shop.

Freda and her sister used to go to Cley beach for picnics. There weren't many cars about then and Freda's first ride in a car was when a commercial traveller took her to Newgate – and she walked back.

A special event in Cley was the Fair, which went to Cley in July. The popular games were Hoop-La and Lucky Dip. One could visit a caravan to see rock being made. Mrs Gizzi was the rock maker (not to be confused with Bill Haley) and she was always very clean.

War broke out in 1914 and the soldiers rallied round. A product at that time was Tinklers Jam and the soldiers used to sing this song:-

> Tinklers Jam, Tinklers Jam,
> How I love old Tinklers Jam
> Plum and apple in one pound pots
> Sent from England in ten ton lots.
> Every night when I'm asleep,

I'm dreaming that I am
Bombing the Huns in the Dardanelles
With Tommy Tinklers Jam!

When Freda's sister (who was ten years older than Freda) was twenty-one, she had a bad illness. The specialist said she must get out as much as possible, so every Thursday (early closing) and Sunday, Freda's mum hired a donkey and trap. Freda had learnt to cycle by then so she went by bike. Neddy (the donkey) was very stubborn and one day they met a car in a narrow lane leading to the coast road at Kelling. Driver of the car stopped to let them pass but Neddy wouldn't go. Eventually the car had to go past – much to everybody's amusement.

There were four pubs in Cley: The Fishmongers, The Mariners Arms, The George and The Swallows and Nightingales. Only The George and The Swallos remain open now.

The local garage was at Blakeney, where the main mechanic was Eddie Hewitt. Blakeney Garage closed and Eddie went as Service Manager to Cley Garage with Vic Firmage as paint-sprayer. Eddie Hewitt was a brilliant mechanic who, when I bought my first car, a white Mini with a black roof – he told my mother that I would be better advised to save up another £50 and get a better Mini. Mum didn't tell me!!!

When I returned from London in 1988 I had a cheque for over £30,000 and wanted to change my Sierra Estate for something newer. Eddie suggested I should go to Cookes of Fakenham and get a VW Passat Estate. Cookes offered me

£2,000 for the Sierra, which was more than I expected. In the yard was a white VW Estate,  C Reg, and a red one, D reg. I chose the red one which I had for twelve years, from1989-2001. Eddie's son, George Hewitt, is a boatbuilder and Repairer on the Old Camp at Stiffkey.

# THE GAZE FAMILY

Egbert Gaze was a corn merchant in North Walsham. His son Philip followed him into the business. Philip married Joyce Davidson, who was born in Swanton Abbot, and they had one son Edmund. Philip died in 1988 and Joyce passed away in 2013.

Edmund (Eddy) was born in 1953. He attended North Walsham Secondary Modern School and then went on to Norwich City College to do a City and Guilds in Electrical Contracting.

Eddy decided he would be better off at Crane Fruehauf than working for an electrical company, so he started there at the age of 19. He moved to Rowlands of Aylsham, making corn bins and hoppers. He took a break from conventional employment for about two years to concentrate on his real love, restoring classic cars.

He started working for North Walsham Plant Hire in1985 and has been there ever since. There have been one or two new owners but Eddy has been there, driving the delivering truck, and maintaining the small machines, for 29 years.

Eddy married in 1977 and had three children, Michael, who is a carpet fitter, Emma, who is a doctors secretary and Sarah, who is a housewife and care assistant.

As mentioned, Eddy's biggest passion   is cars. He enjoys the company of women and likes a drink and a game of pool.

# MORE MOORES

Horace Moore worked on the land and then joined the Royal Navey. On leaving the Navy he worked for the Electricity Board until he retired. I'm afraid I enjoyed this interview but it was difficult because Michael Moore thought he knew a lot.

Horace's son Michael Moore attended Tunstead Junior School and the Hoveton Secondary Modern School. He worked in a coalyard for two weeks and then joined Roys of Wroxham for about a year. He asked Mr Fred Roy if he could be trained for a managerial position. Mr Roy said he would have to go to college and Michael didn't want to do that.

At the age of 22 he got a job laying pipelines in the sea off Gt. Yarmouth, for J.A. Macdermott. The job was somewhat risky and they had to abandon ship twice. Later he was involved in building the oil rigs. They earned good money but they thought they were worth it and also the bonus at the end of a job.

After he left the rigs he became a second-hand car dealer. He is now semi-retired. He does like to hire out the restaurant at the Jolly Farmer's, in Swanton Abbott. If you wish to dine there it is advisable to book.

He said "I could write a book", but so could a lot of people. It's not as easy as it sounds!

# THE HARMER FAMILY

Walter Harmer was born about 1895. He was a lengthman. He looked after some roads around Saxthorpe. He was in the First World War and was a lengthman all his life till he was hit by a car which broke his leg. He developed cancer and died at the age of 62.

George Harmer, Walter's son, was born in 1936 in Saxthorpe. He went to Melton Constable Secondary School, which he left at the oge of 14. He went to Norwich as an apprentice watchmaker. He became a skilled watchmaker and still does it when required.

George was in the RAF for four years at Hemswell, nr Gainsborough, Lincolnshire, where they flew Lancaster bombers. He left the RAF vat the age of 22 and got a job in Holt as a watchmaker with Frank Mayer. He moved on to Wells and worked for John Dawson in Staithe Street. His next step was to move to North Walsham where he worked for John Mears in Mundesley Road.

At the age of 28 George set up his own business as watchmaker in Aylsham.

In 1986, at the age of 50, he retired and set up the "Norfolk Motor Cycle Museum", Rail Yard, near the station at North Walsham.

There is a fine selection of classic motorcycles and scooters and a few old bicycles. The motorcycles are of all makes, mainly British. George's son Steve now runs the business and George, at the age of 78, does a few hours in the afternoon.

George has a sharp sense of humour. I remember when he was in the local shop and said "I think the E.D.P. should be "free" to Old Age Pensioners".

# THETFORD

The woods and heathland around Thetford was the setting for a lot of the recordings of "Dad's Army". Who can forget Captain Mainwaring's faux pas, "Don't tell him, Pike!"?

Corporal Jones, played by that great character actor Clive Dunn, could be relied upon to say "Don't panic", at least once an episode. John Laurie, who played Private Frazer, the undertaker was weird. John was a straight actor who had done some Shakespeare.

Then there was the "public" school educated Sergeant Wilson (John Le Mesurier, who had been married to Hattie Jaques), who thought he was superior to Captain Mainwaring. Throughout the series it was fascinating watching and listening to Captain Mainwaring and Sergeant Wilson. The Captain insisting he was in charge and the Sergeant quietly confident, and know that he could have done the job so much better.

Then there was Walker the spiv (played by James Beck). Jimmy Beck sadly died young. Then Private Godfrey who always wanted to "spend a penny" and the Vicar who seemed to be gay.

# NORFOLK

Norfolk is a very beautiful county, especially for those who are retiring. The North Norfolk Coast is an Area of Outstanding Natural Beauty and then of course we have the ever popular Broads.

Pensthorpe, nr Fakenham has been seen on T.V.'s "Springwatch" and in the summer there are regular trips to see the seals on Blakeney Point. Cromer Pier Theatre has the "Seaside Special" season and then there is the largest seaside town in Norfolk, Gt. Yarmouth.

The North Norfolk Railway, the "Poppy Line" has steam trains running from Sheringham to Holt. Norfolk Lavender at Heacham is a popular attraction and Thursford is famous for its Christmas shows.

King's Lynn, or Bishop's Lynn, as it used to be called, is an interesting town. It is still a port positioned on the Great Ouse River. It has a big market on Tuesdays and a good shopping centre.

Walsingham is a place of Pilgrimage, and Norfolk has many churches with round towers, built of Norfolk flint.

Of course Norfolk's city is Norwich, with easy access to London by train. It has an airport and a football team nicknamed "The Canaries", they play in Yellow and Green. It has the University of East Anglia and the Norfolk & Norwich

University Hospital nearby. Norwich has the studios for local news both on B.B.C. and I.T.V.

Norfolk is the third largest county in England, after Yorkshire and Lincolnshire. It is quite flat and has some "big" skies.

# SANDRINGHAM

Sandringham House is where the Royal Family regularly spend Christmas. It was bought in the 19<sup>th</sup> century by Prince Edward, Prince of Wales. Lord Palmerston arranged it, the purchase price was £220,000.

Queen Victoria was more keen on Balmoral and Osborne House, on the Isle of Wight. But after her death Edward VII, George V and George VI loved Sandringham which is one reason why it is so dear to Queen Elizabeth II.

In the grounds of the Sandringham Estate is Park House. Lady Diana Spencer, later Princess Diana, spent some of her childhood at Park House.

The Royal Family used to travel by train to Wolferton Station, before the King's Lynn to Hunstanton line was done away with. Now they either travel to King's Lynn by train and then car or by car all the way from London.

The Sandringham Estate covers 8,000 hectares. There are 240 hectares of woodland and heath. The estate includes tidal mudflats, woodland and wetland, arable, livestock and fruit farms. The visitor centre is open all the year round – there is a free car park – and the gift shop and plant shop are very interesting.

Not far from Park House is the Sandringham Cricket Ground. In about 1963 Sandringham were at home to Stiffkey. In the

Sandringham team was John Barrett, who would later go on to play for Norfolk. Sandringham batted first and made180 odd before tea.

After tea Mark Jarvis and Allan Tuck opened for Stiffkey. Allan was out ealy and Anthony (Tom) Sands went in at No.3. Runs flowed freely and Stiffkey won by 9   wickets. Mark made a steady 40 not out and Tom had hit a magnificent century. I know, I was doing the scorebook.

Sandringham is a good cricket pitch but the best in the area is at Anmer.

When the Royals are in residence the Queen visits Sandringham W.I., of which she is President.

# NORFOLK CRICKET

Ingham, near Stalham, used to stage a match between an Edrich XI and the Lord's Taveners.

The Edrich XI was, obviously, made up of the Edrich family. The Lord's Taveners were made up of stars of entertainment and good cricketers.

I went to a match where Mr Pastry (Richard Hearne), Peter May, Roya Castle and many others were playing.

Norfolk C.C. used to play at Lakenham in Norwich, where I went for my "trial". Now the county play at Horsford, near the junction of the Norwich/Holt and Norwich/Cromer roads.

Henry Blofield, the radio "5 Live Extra" commentator, used to be the Norfolk wicket keeper. Geoff Green, who was still at Fakenham Grammer School, played for Norfolk. He later went to work for Vauxhall, in Luton, and tested their cars round Brands Hatch, in Kent. Geoff must have been going too fast, when he was returning from Luton to Guist, to visit the family for the weekend, when he turned his car over and was killed.

Cromer C.C. has a nice ground, although rather small. Many sixes are hit at Cromer. Ian Mercer, Graham Witton, Philip Mindham, Walter Elliott and Tony Laws, who was also groundsman have all played for Cromer.

# PUBS

Many Public Houses have closed down. The Railway Tavern has shut it's doors. A few years under Marlene and Gary Thompson it was a good pub, with darts and cribbage teams, and the base of the "Holt Flyer". The "Holt Flyer" was a horse and carriage that carried people from Holt Station (in High Kelling) to the town centre, and back again.

Marlene and Gary decided to move to France. Joan Wainwright had her 90th Birthday party there, where she received her ideal gift – her own keg of Guinness (88 pints).

The Three Horseshoes at Scottow has closed, as has the Railway at Coltishall. Even some pubs on the coast have shut – the Ship at Bacton.

Years ago the village pub was the regular meeting place for people who "needed people". First of all came the motor car, which meant people could travel about, and they tended to leave the villages and go into "town". Then came television, which meant people were entertained in the comfort of their own homes.

People were encouraged to drink less, not to drink and drive, and with the supermarkets selling "cheap" cans or bottles, it was more economical to drink at home.

There used to be arguments about what to watch on T.V.. Now this is less of a problem with D.V.D's to record programmes, and lots of houses having more than one T.V.

I had a colour portable T.V. that my mother bought me as a present. I "sold" it to a man for his step-children, but never got paid for it.

Wells-next-the-Sea is an example of a town that has lost most of its pubs. The Eight Ringers, the Park Tavern, the Ship Inn, the Shipwrights Arms, have all closed.

The Edinburgh, Golden Fleece, Ark Royal, the Crown, the Globe are all that remain. Of course there are lots of restaurants,

I think the point is there is a lot of money in Norfolk, so people tend not to go out for a drink, they go out to lunch or dinner, or, if you are posh, supper, as in Castle Acre.

There is usually work for chefs, waiters and waitresses, in the area. In fact in the Hanser, in Stalham Green, it is very reasonable. I think this is because they have a minimum number of staff. There is a barman/waiter, and a cook/chef, who I believe is female. You can get a good meal in the Hanser for £7 or £8.

# SIR WILLIAM PASTON

William Paston went to Corpus Christie College, Cambridge at the age of fourteen. He left in 1627, being able to speak several languages – but he did love his recreation, and played a lot of tennis.

William married Lady Katherine Butie, a daughter of Robert, 1$^{st}$ Earl of Lindsey.

A few years later the English Civil War broke out. William and Katherine were opposed to the Puritan outlook in matters of church and state.

They loved art. Van Dyke painted the Queen, Rubens adorned the Banqueting House at Whitehall with great canvases, which displayed the monarchy driving back rebellion and envy.

Lady Katherine had given birth to three sons and two daughters. In 1637 she died giving birth to their sixth child. In 1637 William served as High Sheriff of Norfolk. After that William travelled a lot, he visited Italy, Egypt and Jerusalem.

1640 was a terrible year for the English. The King had not created any new baronets in Norfolk for twelve years, but in 1641 he created several, some of whom opposed him.

It was about this time that William married his second wife, Margaret Hewitt, daughter of Sir Thomas Hewitt of Pishiobury in Hertfordshire.

Sir William then spent a lot of time in Holland, but on the 14<sup>th</sup> June 1643 the House of Commons made an order that Sir William Paston and eleven other gentleman from Norfolk and Suffolk, shall at once be required to return to England otherwise all their estates, real and personal, shall be sequestered and employed for the service of the Commonwealth. Paston ignored this and his estates were duly taken away. He returned to England to try to get these back and on 3<sup>rd</sup> June 1644 they were discharged.

On 22<sup>nd</sup> February 1663 he died. A few days later he was buried at Oxnead.

There is a portrait of Sir William Paston at the Paston College in North Walsham.

# WEST NORFOLK

Hunstanton is a fascinating town. It has a lovely green in front of what used to be the pier. To the north the cliffs are layered chalk and carrstone – a bit like "ice cream".

The funfair is to the south of the main town but there are arcades where slot machines abound. Fish and chips are readily available but so are other lunches and dinners at the many pubs and hotels.

To the north of the town is a lighthouse and as we turn eastwards we find Hunstanton Golf Course, which is a good test of players ability.

Further along the coast is Titchwell Nature Reserve and in Brancaster – The Royal West Norfolk Golf Club, with its deep bunkers and deadly rough.

Slightly inland is the beautiful small town of Burnham Market, which is popular with Londoners and stars of Television. Then there is the attractive sailing village of Burnham Overy Staithe.

Next is Holkham, famous for the Hall, the grounds of which contain a cricket pitch, a lake and a deer park. At the junction of the road from the Hall to the A149 is the Victoria Pub, and, over the road, towards the sea, a road leading to the miles of sand that is Holkham Bay. A mile further along we find Wells-next-the-Sea, where work and pleasure meet. There are some fishing boats and some sailing yachts and cruisers. Wells is another town that has suffered due to the closing down of the rail link to Norwich. It is quite popular with the locals who enjoy eating fish and chips on the small wall by the quay.

Inland from Wells we have the village of Walsingham, which pilgrims visit every Easter. Further inland is Fakenham which has a lively market on Thursdays, an auction house, several supermarkets and a National Hunt Racecourse. Interlinked with the Racecourse is Fakenhams nine-hole golf course.

If we leave Fakenham on the B1146 we pass the Gressenhall Rural Life Museum en route to Dereham. Dereham boasts a good shopping centre and is on the reconstructed Mid-Norfolk Railway, which goes to Wymondham. This is a line restored by enthusiasts on part of the old route from Wells to Norwich.

Going west from Dereham we come to Swaffham, which has a thriving market on a Saturday. Southwest is Cockley Cley, the Iceni Village and Museum, Gooderstone Water Gardens and Oxburgh Hall.

Further west is Downham Market on the Great Ouse and the main line from King's Lynn to King's Cross. Finally we come round to the largest town in West Norfolk, King's Lynn.

In the Doomsday Book, Bishop's Lynn (as it was known) was little more than a village. By the early 13th century Lynn had become a thriving market town. By 1204, when Lynn received its first Royal Charter, it was the fourth port of the Kingdom.

The rapid development of Bishop's Lynn led to the foundation of two Chapels-of-Ease to St Margaret's – St James (1130) and St Nicholas (1146) and the friars were established in the Wash port before 1300.

Lynn's importance grew in the Middle Ages because of its standing on the Great Ouse. It was in a good position on the East Coast, giving easy access to London and Scotland, and to Europe, across the North Sea.

Herring, furs, wax, timber, iron and pitch were imported, and cloth, skins, wool, salt and lead were exported to Baltic harbours, by Lynn and Hanseatic ships.

Lynn's exports paid for the importation of lots of wine from south-west France in the 13th and 14th centuries.

By the time of the Black Death in 1348, Lynn's population had grown to about 10,000. Approximately half of England's five million inhabitants died. Lynn soon recovered and by 1388 fifty-nine Neighbourhood Guilds had been formed.

King John reportedly lost his baggage train and jewels in the Wash. A dejected and ill monarch continued via Wisbech but died at Newark.

Throughout the centuries King's Lynn was an important port for exports, mainly corn. East Anglia is still a big producer of corn but much of it is now used in this country, and transported by road.

An important new development near King's Lynn is the Palm Paper Mill. About 1000 tonnes of waste paper daily is transported to the plant from over East Anglia. Leaving the plant every day are 60 or more lorry loads of newsprint on giant rolls to feed the presses of various newspaper groups. The plant employs about 150 people.

# THE PARSON WOODFORDE

The Parson Woodforde, Freehouse and Restaurant, in Weston Longville, has a solid oak front door. The building dates back to 1827 and opened as a Freehouse in 1845, called the Five Ringers.

James Woodforde was born in 1740 at the Parsonage in Somerset, the son of Reverand Samual Woodforde, Rector of Ansford and Vicar of Castle Cary.

He left Somerset to study at Oxford in 1758 and later became a Fellow and Sub-Warden of the New College which led him to Weston Longville, Norfolk when he obtained a college living in 1774. He lived with his niece, Nancy, who acted as housekeeper, and he never married.

For nearly 45 years he kept a diary, with almost daily entries, recording his relatively ordinary life in 18th century rural England.

He made his first diary entry on 21$^{st}$ July 1759: *"Made a Scholar of New-College"* and his last entry on 17$^{th}$ October 1802 just before he passed away in January 1803: *"We breakfasted, dined, Very weak this Morning, scarce able to put on my Cloaths and with great difficulty, get down Stairs with help – Mr Dade read Prayers and Preached this Morning at Weston Church – Nancy at Church – Mr and Mrs Custance & Lady Bacon at Church – Dinner today Rost Beef &c*

The Parson's love for good food and drink shines through in his entries and comments *"Eat and drink I can very well & with an Appetite"* (25th May 1802) He would often indulge in fine dining *"Dinner to day, Cod-Fish & Oysters & Shrimp Sauce and a couple of Partridges rosted &c"*. (9th November 1800) and enjoyed brewing his own beer, *"Made a Barrel of Mead to day, about 19. Pounds of Honey to six Gallons of Water, some few Races of Ginger and a Handfull of dried Elder Flowers put in a fine Holland Cloth & boiled with it."*(12th November 1795).

His love of Norfolk was also apparent in his diaries, *We breakfasted, dined, supped and slept at Norwich. We took a walk over to the City in the morning, and we both agreed that it was the finest City in England by far"* (14th April 1775).

What better way to honour the Parsons memory than to name a Freehouse and Restaurant after him that enjoys all the same things! The Parsons love of fine food, great ale and the local area are all celebrated at The Parson Woodforde.

James Woodfordes diaries first came to light when John Beresford edited a five-volume abridgement in the 1920's and since then people have become endeared by the Parson. The Parson Woodforde Society was established in 1968 by Revd Canon L Rule Wilson for enthusiasts to learn more about James Woodforde's life, the society in which he lived and to visit places associated with the diarist.

Extracts from Parson Woodfordes' Diary:-

Dec 3$^{rd}$ 1779 – *"Nancy began trying Goulard Tincture tonight (on her painful knee) I hope it will be of service to her with God's Blessings"*

Dec 4$^{th}$ 1779 – *"This evening by Mr Cary came Bill's present to me, viz a large Moorish Sword and a curious Moors Purse made of Morocco Leather with some coins in it. He also sent me two curious shells and a quill that came from Falklands Island. It is some gratitude to him I must confess – but he expects something in return as he complains in his letter to me of being very low in Pocket."*

Dec 6$^{th}$ 1779 – *"At Quadrille this evening, won £0.1.0d. Gave Nancy for cards as she had very bad luck £0.5.0d. Nancy thinks the Goulard does her good already."*

Dec 15$^{th}$ 1779 – *"My Squire (Mr Custance) sent me over a note this morning to let me know that his Lady was brought to bed of a son in the afternoon yesterday...I dressed myself and rode over to Ringland upon my mare by myself about 12 and privately baptised the child by name George. Mrs Custace was as well as could be expected."*

Dec 18th 1779 – *"Very busy all the morning in putting up a hand pump into the Dyke by my great  Pond to endeavour to raise the water on my pond higher – after many alterations of the pump we at last made it answer. Mr Pyle was here most of the day, employed on it. Mr Pyle dined here etc. And I paid him a long bill respecting my Chancel of £28.12.0. In the*

*Norwich paper this evening I saw my name put down to preach a Charity Sermon at St Stephens Norwich, the 16<sup>th</sup> April next.*

# THE SHERINGHAM LIFEBOATS

In 1838 the first Sheringham Lifeboat, the "Augusta" was launched. It was paid for by the Hon. Charlotte Upcher of Sheringham Hall. "Augusta" was the name of Mrs Upchers youngest child.

If you drive through Upper Sheringham now there is a trickle of water across the road near the church. This stream used to be much bigger and the "Augusta" was launched from Sheringham Hall and went to sea by this route.

It was built by Robert Sunman for £134.12s.2d and was fitted with sixteen oars. The "Augusta" was in service for 56 years, from 1838-1894 and during this time had only two coxswains, Robert Long from 1838-1859, and Tom Barnes Cooper from 1859-1894.

In 1867 the R.N.L.I. introduced their own lifeboat to Sheringham, called "The Duncan". It was built by Forestt of Limehouse for £345. It was paid for by Mrs Agnes Fraser (nee Duncan) in memory of her father and uncle. So between 1867 and 1886 Sheringham had two lifeboats. Coxwains of "The Duncan" were Edmund Pye West (1867-1868), John Grace (1869), William "Buck" Craske (1870-1873), Abraham Cooper (1874) and Robert "Philopoo" Cooper (1875-1886)

The next lifeboat was the "Henry Ramsey Upcher", donated by Mrs Cathering Upcher of Sheringham Hall, in memory of her husband. It was built by Lewis "Buffalo" Emery of

Sheringham for £1509, in the style of the local crab boats. It was in service from 1894-1935. Coxwains of the "Henry Ramsey Upcher" were Tom Barnes Cooper (1894-1898), "Old Coley" Cooper (1898-1935).

The "J.C. Madge" was in service from 1904 – 1936. It was built by the Thames Ironworks Shipbuilding Co. Ltd, Blackwall for £1436.

The "J.C. Madge" was launched 34 times, saving 58 lives. The coxswains were William "Click" Bishop (1904-1914), Obadiah Cooper (1914-1924) and James Dumble (1924-1936).

The "Foresters' Centenary" was built by Groves and Gutteridge, Isle of Wight, at a cost of £3569. It was fitted with a 35 hp petrol engine. It was launched 129 times, saving 82 lives, and stayed in service until 1967. Coxwains of the "Foresters' Centenary" were James Dumble (1936-1947), Sparrow Hardingham (1947-1950) and Henry "Downtide" West (1951-1961.

The "Manchester Unity of Oddfellows" (1961-1990) was built by William Osborne's shipyard, Littlehampton and cost £28,500. Between 1961 and 1990 it was launched 127 times, saving 134 lives. Coxwains of the "Manchester Unity of Oddfellows" were Henry Downtide" West (1961-1962), Henry "Joyful" West (1963-1984), Jack West (1985-1986), Brian Pegg (1986-1989) and Clive Rayment (1989-1990). Several temporary lifeboats saw service between 1990 and

1994 before the Atlantic 75 – "Manchester Unity of Oddfellows" took over in 1994.

# BEAUTIFUL NORFOLK

Norfolk was ignored as a picturesque place for a long time. The Lakes, The Peak, Dovedale, the Wye Valley, the Southern Coast and parts of Wales were more obviously beautiful.

Humphrey Repton, who toured Norfolk in about 1780, wrote about the vast spreading distances, the rich arable lands, the leafy hedgerows, a prodigious softness to the landscape, then there were wonderful skies, light and cloud.

Houghton, Holkham, Blickling, Raynham, Wolterton and Narford drew people from London and elsewhere. Also Oxnead, a home of the Paston family, but no longer in existence.

Years later people began to appreciate the countryside. They travelled through the county looking at beauty, the delightful tract of land around Bayfield and Letheringsett, with its trees and the River Glaven. The journey from Holt to Cromer was memorable – the sea always in view – fishing boats and colliers from Newcastle to London.

The Norwich School of Art came to appreciate Norfolk – led by John Crome (1782-1821), John Thirtle (1777-1839) and John Sell Cotman (1782-1842).

In 1803 John Crome founded the Norwich Society of Artists. He painted Carrow Abbey and The Yare at Thorpe.

He achieved a freshness of vision and colour that is comparable to Constable's magnificent painting of the next twenty years. He also did some sensitive etchings which were published after his death.

Crome's son, John Berney Crome (1742-1842) was the best artist of his four children. His most famous work was the "Yarmouth Water Frolick"

James Stark (1794-1859) was a follower of Crome. He painted "Sheep Washing" and in about 1835 "Cromer".

Of all Crome's pupils, the most accomplished was George Vincent (1796-1832). He painted "Trowse Meadows near Norwich" and "Dutch Fair on Yarmouth Beach".

John Berney Ladbrook (1803-1879) carried the Norwich School landscapes into the Victorian era. He painted "A Lane Scene" and "A Woodland Scene".

Probably the most famous member of the Norwich School of Art was John Sell Cotman. He travelled round Britain before returning to Norwich in 1805. He etched "Walsingham Abbey Gate" and painted "The Marl Pit" about 1809 and "The Mars – riding off Anchor off Cromer" in 1807. Most of his work was in watercolour but his oil of "Silver Birches" is outstanding.

John Sell Cotman's sons, Miles Edmund Cotman and John Joseph Cotman were both artists, the latter painted "Norwich Castle", "Trowse Meadows, Norwich" and "Figures in Landscape".

Henry Bright (1810-1873) was another important Norwich artist with "Windmill at Sheringham" and "North Beach, Gt Yarmouth" in the early 1840's.

The coming of the railways during Victorian times proved to be a boon to Norfolk. Visitors rushed to the coast for their holidays. Norfolk was within reasonably easy reach of Londoners and people from the Midlands. Some Londoners settled on Southend but for the inhabitants of the East Midlands towns Norfolk was the shortest trip to the coast. There was a Leicester week and a Nottingham week, and Hunstanton, Cromer and Gt Yarmouth were the obvious destinations. These days you can still get to Cromer and Gt Yarmouth by train, changing at Norwich, but now one cannot get to Hunstanton.

The smaller towns also benefited from the railways. People could get to Heacham, Wells-next-the-Sea, Sheringham, Mundesley and Wroxham for the Norfolk Broads The Broads is still a popular venue for tourists but of course now most of the boats have engines rather than sails or oars.

At the beginning of the 20th Century came the motor car – but of course to start with only rich people could afford one. Norfolk has never been at the forefront when roads have been built. The A149 from King's Lynn to Hunstanton has been improved, also the A148 from King's Lynn to Cromer. Comparatively recently the A47 Southern Bypass round Norwich has been completed and the duelling of the A11 from Thetford to Barton Mills is new. But the nearest motorway is the M11 at Cambridge.

Nowadays, North Norfolk is an Area of Outstanding Natural Beauty. The A149 coast road from Cromer to Hunstanton is staying as it was as the visitors like to enjoy the scenery. To get from Cromer to Hunstanton quickly you have to use the A148 to Holt and Fakenham and then turn off to Docking and Heacham, near Norfolk Lavender, and approach Hunstanton from the south. Hunstanton is the answer to a regularly asked quiz question – Which is the only seaside resort in the East that faces West? The popularity of Hunstanton has declined since the rail link with King's Lynn is no more.

# METHODISTS IN EAST NORFOLK

North Walsham Church of England church is unusual insomuch as it only has part of its tower. Some of it collapsed in 1724.

But we are concerned here with Methodists, Methodism was started by the brothers John and Charles Wesley, in the 18$^{th}$ century.

Bringing Methodism to Gt. Yarmouth was not easy. It was an un-Godly place. In 1754 Mr Thomas Olivers and a companion travelled from Norwich on horseback, and after attending the parish church, went to the Market Place. A crowd gathered and as Mr Olivers started his sermon the crowd began to attack him. They managed to escape and after sheltering in the Rows they had sticks, stones, turnips and potatoes thrown at them.

In 1760, Captain Howell Harris had different ideas. He led a group of soldiers into Gt. Yarmouth. He was close friends with many leading Methodists, John and Charles Wesley, George Whitefield and the Countess of Huntingdon. He reached the Market Place and stated that a Methodist preacher would address the crowd. He stood on a table and with his soldiers backing him up, they sang a hymn. Then Captain Harris started to preach. The crowd would take no action due to the threat from the soldiers. This was a turning point for Methodism in Gt. Yarmouth.

There were several breakaway groups from the Wesleyan Methodists. The "Kilhamites", the "Society of Primitive Methodists", later the "Bible Christian Society" was formed in 1815 and the "Protestant Methodists" in 1827. Finally in 1849, another group broke away to form the "Wesleyan Reform Movement".

In 1857 the breakaway movements started to unite and finally in 1932 the Methodist Church was back as we know it today.

We are covering an area of East Norfolk from Gt. Yarmouth and Gorleston in the East, up to Sutton, near Stalham in the North and across to Lingwood in the West.

The breakaway groups had built their own churches and sometimes there were two in a village. People didn't want to leave one church and go to another. However, during the Second World War many were destroyed.

Since the War many churches have become less popular, especially in the villages, and have been sold off. One or two have become bric-a-brac shops.

# NORFOLK FLINT

Grimes Graves are a series of caves in South-West Norfolk where flint was mined. They are a popular tourist attraction and one of the few places in Norfolk where you can go "underground".

In parts of Norfolk the chalk strata is up to 300m thick. It is in the chalk strata that flint in its natural state appears.

Flint was used in building churches, and in particular round church towers. There are about 170 round church towers in East Anglia, and only      six in the rest of England. In some cases octagonal belfries were added to circular churh towers. Flint is composed almost entirely of Silica.

Flints can occur in many places. On Sheringham beach there are flints that are "rounded" by the action of the sea.

Flint was used to build many houses in Norfolk. Building a house with flints took considerable skill. Bricklaying is relatively easy because the bricks are flat and of standard size, whereas flints are all sorts of shapes and require a lot of mortar to knot them into a wall. Nowadays it is very unusual for a house to be built of flints.

But flint walls can be quite popular. However, when building with flint a builder really earns his money.

# ROGER LLOYD PACK

Roger Lloyd Pack was born into a theatrical family. His father was Charles Lloyd Pack, a serious actor.

Roger was a fine straight actor, and had appeared in many programmes on television.

However, he will be best remembered for his character "Trigger" in "Only Fools and Horses" and farmer Owen Nevitt in "The Vicar of Dibley".

He loved Norfolk and lived in a cottage in Hindolveston, near Melton Constable.

Trigger had his own ways in "Only Fools and Horses" where he always called Rodney "Dave". He had never had a new broom from the council, just fourteen heads and ten shafts. He was also present in the bar when Del Boy was trying to impress the ladies and fell over when the flap of the bar was left up. Trigger couldn't work out where Del Boy had gone.

As Owen Nevitt he was nearly always late for the meetings chaired by Mr Horton. He always had a problem on the farm. He sometimes had his arm halfway up a cows backside or he was knee deep in slurry. Owen fancied Rev. Geraldine Grainger (played by Dawn French) but Geraldine had her thoughts on higher (and cleaner) things.

Roger was remarkable because his deadpan expression showed us he was taking things very seriously, although he made millions of us laugh.

He will be greatly missed.

# CROMER PIER

Cromer Pier houses the Theatre that does "Seaside Specials" and also the Lifeboat House, between the theatre and the sea. It was built in 1901 and in 1905 a bandstand was added.

Summer Seasons started and continued until the outbreak of the Second World War, when the Royal Engineers removed the middle section of the pier.

Shows resumed after the war. The pier and pavilion were seriously damaged in the great styorm of 1953, but the pier re-opened in 1955. In 1978 the theatre was refurbished and the popular "Seaside Specials" began.

Many stars have visited Cromer Pier Theatre:-

Including:- 1937 – ROB WILTON
    1938 – WEE GEORGIE WOOD, VIC OLIVER
    1957- CHRIS BARBER
    1960 – SEMPRINI, BRYAN JOHNSON
    1961 – PETER BROUGH AND ARCHIE ANDREWS
    1964 – DAVID JACOBS
    1973 – WALTER LANDAUER, BILL PERTWEE
    1978 – HUMPHREY LITTLETON
    1978 – RICHARD DIGANCE
    1980 – ACKER BILK
    1983 – THE TEMPERANCE SEVEN
    1987 – MAX JAFFA
    1989 – VAL DOONICAN

1997 – MAX BYGRAVES, DANNY LA RUE

1998 – PAUL DANIELS

One of the best "seaside Specials" was when "Tucker" starred. He is a comedian but in the second half he sang the song "The Wonder of You" or was he miming?

A new bar and restaurant were added in 2004. In late 2013 the pier suffered damage again through storms and tide but it has been repaired and is ready for the 2014 "Seaside Special".

# NORWICH CITY FOOTBALL CLUB

Norwich City Football Club was formed at a meeting in the Criterion Cafe in White Lion Street in the summer of 1902. The new Norwich City F.C. played at Newmarket Road and gained admission to the Norfolk and Suffolk League. The first match took place against Harwich which ended in a 1-1 draw.

City wore blue and white and were known as the Citizens. By 1905 they  won  the regional league title but were in trouble for paying players travelling expenses etc. They decided to turn professional and enter the Southern League.

Enthusiastic fans adopted ther anthem "On the Ball City" and a local pastime of breeding canaries, caused a club nickname to become "The Canaries", and the colours were changed to yellow and green.

A new ground had to be found and the Canaries settled in "The Nest" in Rosary Road. This happened in 1908 and the first match was a friendly with Fulham.

After the 1914-18 war the Football League introduced Third Division (South) and Third Division (North). Norwich were invited to join the Third Division (South) in 1920. Crowds were growing and "The Nest" wasn't big enough. The Colman Company offered the Carrow Road site and Norwich moved there in 1935.

City struggled after the Second World War, twice having to apply for re-election. In the early 1950's form was improving and several notable cup victories were gained. 1958/59 was one of the Canaries' greatest seasons. They beat Ilford 3-1 in the first round of the F.A. Cup.

Then they beat Manchester United 3-0 at Carrow Road and next Cardiff were overcome 3-2. They drew at Tottenham and won the replay. They battled to force a replay with Sheffield United, where keeper Ken Nethercott dislocated his shoulder. They won the replay 3-2 with Sandy Kennon in goal.

They were through to the semi-finals of the F.A. Cup. They drew 1-1 with Luton Town at White Hart Lane but lost the replay 1-0 at St Andrews, Birmingham. They won the Sunday Pictorial "Giant Killer" Cup.

Manager Archie Macauley took them up to Division Two 1960 and then the Canaries won the League Cup, beating Rochdale over two legs in the final. Captain Ron Ashman lifted the trophy in triumph.

More good cup victories followed before manager Ron Saunders took Norwich City into the First Division in April 1972.

In August 1972-73, in the top division Norwich's first game was at home to Everton which resulted in a 1-1 draw, Jimmy Bone getting the Norwich goal. In 1973 Norwich reached the league Cup Final but lost 1-0 to Tottenham. In 1975 the

Canaries again reached the league Cup Final only to lose to Aston Villa 1-0. It was third time lucky in 1985 when Norwich beat Sunderland 1-0. A deflected shot by Asa Hartford securing the victory.

In the same year Norwich were relegated to Division Two. As a result of their League Cup victory Norwich should have gone into Europe but because of the problems at the Hysel stadium English clubs were banned from Europe. In 1985-86 Norwich returned to the First Division as Champions of League Two.

1988-89 was a very good season for the Canaries. They finished well up the league and reached the semi-final of the F.A. Cup when they lost 1-0 to Everton at Villa Park. They missed Robert Fleck whose father had died on the Friday causing him to rush off to Scotland. This semi-final was the same day as the tragedy at Hillsborough.

In 1991-92 Norwich reached their third F.A. Cup semi-final losing 1-0 to Sunderland at Hillsborough.

In 1992-93 the Premier League started and, under manager Mike Walker Norwich finished third, their best ever position. They went into Europe in the U.E.F.A. Cup and beat Bayern Munich with a classic strike from Jeremy Goss.

1995 saw Norwich relegated to the Championship but were promoted back to the Premiership in 2003-04. In 2004-05 they were relegated again and in 2009 they were relegated again down to Division One. Bryan Gunn was replaced by

Paul Lambert who immediately brought City back to the Championship and, straight through, the following season, to the Premiership.

Paul Lambert decided to go to Aston Villa and Chris Houghton became the Norwich manager. He took them to a mid-table position in 2012-13.

Quite a lot of money was spent in the summer of 2013. Ricky Van Wolfswinkle arrived for £8.5 million.

When I visited the club on 12$^{th}$ February 2014, there was much concern about the league position but most of the staff were confident we would avoid relegation.

Over the years Norwich City has been served by some very good players – Johnny Gavin, Joe Hannah, Terry Bly, Terry Allcock, Ron Ashman, Duncan Forbes, David Stringer, David Cross, Graham Paddon (who scored a fantastic hat-trick when Norwich won 3-0 at Arsenal), Ted Macdougall, Phil Boyer, Mike Phelan, Andy Townshend, Dave Bowen, Andy Linigan, Robert Fleck, David Phillips, Dale Gordon, Micky Adams, Peter Crouch, Malky Mackay, Darren Huckersby and Grant Holt.

The club has been particularly well served by some very fine goalkeepers, Ken Nethercott, Sandy Kennon, the very agile Kevin Keegan, Chris Woods, Bryan Gunn and John Ruddy.

# "BILLY" QUANTRILL

"Billy! Quantrill was well known as a local footballer. He was born in 1945 in Wetherby, Yorkshire but the family moved to Norfolk and went to Lingwood Junior School, near Norwich. Another move took the family to Mundesley and Billy went to North Walsham Secondary Modern School. On leaving school he went to Easton College to learn farm management. When Billy left college he went to work for Charlie Payne on a farm in Mundesley.

While at North Walsham School Billy was made captain of the junior team (U.13) and then he progressed to captain of the senior team. He was a prefect. Billy also helped the P.E. master to coach the younger boys. He played for East Norfolk Schoolboys and played rugby for Norfolk Schoolboys

When Billy left school his dad had an offer to send him as an apprentice footballer to Arsenal F.C. However, Billy's dad didn't tell him, he wanted Billy to have a "proper" job, on the farm, and go to Easton College, which he did.

At Easton College Billy played Soccer, Rugby and Cricket.

When he left college Billy played football for North Walsham in the Norfolk and Suffolk League. The Anglian Combination was formed and Billy moved to Overstrand F.C., where he spent 18 years, from the age of 18 to 36. He also played in the Norwich Sunday League and his last season at the age of 34 he scored 9 hat-tricks in    9 games, a lot with his head.

Billy worked at Payne's for six years until he was 24, when he moved to Crane Fruehauf in North Walsham, where he stayed for 20 years from 1969-1989. He started as a storeman and ended up as a supervisor on the production line.

At the age of 36 Billy left Overstrand F.C. and played for Cromer for 2 years. Then he went to Dilham where he played till he was 47. He went on the Physiotherapy Course (Sports Injuries) at Carrow Road, Norwich and became Assistant Manager and Physio at North Walsham F.C.

For personal reasons Billy left football at the age of 54 and took up golf at Mundesley Golf Club. He was elected Vice-Captain in 2012 and Captain in 2013.

Billy Quantrill got married one Saturday morning, played football in the afternoon, and went on Honeymoon Saturday evening. That was a busy day.

# THE GOOD OLD DAYS?

In Norfolk, as in the rest of the country, at the beginning of the twentieth century, very few people had cars. You had to be quite rich. It was common for people to bike 20-30 miles.

The main employment for "poor" women was in service – either as a helper to one lady or part of a team working "below stairs" in a big house.

Servants would include a butler, a cook, a lady's maid, a valet, a footman and possibly a chauffer. The driving test was not introduced until 1934, so I suppose if you showed a potential employer that you could handle a vehicle, you may have gotten the job.

Many men worked on the land, as farm labourers, for very low wages, if you couldn't manage the only place to go was the workhouse. There are many workhouses still in existence, usually converted to houses or flats.

The First World War changed all of that. The young men went to fight (and possibly die) for their country, which left the young women to look after things at home. Many tended the land or worked in munitions factories, making weapons and bullets for the troops.

After the War and the work of the Suffragettes the role of women became more recognised. They got the vote and were considered to be as "good" as men.

# PETER PARFITT

Peter Parfitt attended Fakenham Grammer School at about the same time as Anthony (Tom) Sands.

Some say Tom was the better cricketer than Peter but he didn't want a cricketing career.

Peter played for the school, obviously, and went on to play for Middlesex. He was a contemporary of John Murray, Freddie Titmas and John Price – who all played for Midddlesex and England. John Price opened the bowling. He was a mountain of a man, about 6ft 3ins tall and broad with it.

Peter tells the story of when he was 12<sup>th</sup> man for Middlesex and Denis Compton, a brilliant batsman in the late 1940's (at the same time as Bill Edrich) arrived at Lords. He had obviously not been home because he was still wearing his dinner suit.

"Can you find me something to wear?" Compton asked Parfitt. Peter had a look round the pavilion and found some clothing – which didn't really fit, but it would do.

"Can you find me a bit of wood, Twelfthers?" asked Compton. Peter found his a bat.

When it was Compton's turn to bat he went in and made a century. It just goes to show that it doesn't matter what you wear, providing you have the ....... talent.

Peter went on to play many times for England. He was a left-handed bat, who bowled occasionally, and an excellent close to the wicket fielder.

Tom Sands worked for North Norfolk District Council in Cromer, he still lives in Wells. He had captained one of the better Holt Football Club sides. He was a commanding centre-half. He played the occasional game of cricket for his home village, Stiffkey.

# Mr. S. ECKERSLEY

Stanley Eckersley (nicknamed Nats – Stan backwards) took over as headmaster of Fakenham Grammer School in 1939. He was to stay there for thirty years until his retirement in 1968.

Fakenham Grammer School was founded in 1923 and up to 1968 the school had only had two headmasters.

Mr Eckersley was like a father figure, firm but fair. He had a sense of humour but he didn't suffer fools gladly.

During his stay at F.G.S. Mr Eckersley saw many changes. A new wing was built, a new science lab and a swimming pool. To many pupils regret the swimming pool was not covered until after Mr Eckersley retired. Many great academic and sporting achievements occurred during his time, including the education of our most famous old boy, Peter Parfitt. (see another chapter.)

Mr Eckersley worked very hard. He taught only one subject, Economic and Public Affairs (Politics) at "A" level. But he did so much other work. He arranged the timetables and tried to get pupils to the right place at the right time.

I still remember something he said, "You know the old saying – honesty is the best policy. Well policies are what political parties have ---Honesty in a principle."

There is a road in Fakenham called Eckersley Drive, named after this outstanding man.

# R.A.F. COLTISHALL

R.A.F.Coltishall – about eight miles north of Norwich was built in 1939 and 1940. It was to be called R.A.F. Buxton after the nearest railway station, but this may have been confused with Buxton in Derbyshire, so it became R.A.F. Coltishgall. The first flight took place in 1940, a Bristol Blenheim IVL 7835 flown by Sergeant R.G. Bales, and Sergeant Barnes.

During the Second World War, Coltishall was home to the Hawker Hurricane and a notable fighter pilot was Douglas Bader – the man who had his legs rebuilt. Bader has a road named after him in North Walsham. A film was made about Bader called "Reach for the Sky", starring that splendid actor, Kenneth More.

From 10th February to 7th April 1945 it was the home of No.124 Squadron R.A.F., at that time a fighter bomber squadron flying Supermarine Spitfire 1XHF's while the squadron was bombing V2 launch sites in Holland. As the war ended R.A.F. Coltishall was briefly given over to Polish squadrons until they returned home.

In the 1950's R.A.F. Coltishall was a designated "V Bomber dispersal airfield". This was our "Nuclear Detterent" – the Avro Vulcan, Handley Page Victor and the Vickers Valient.

Since the war R.A.F. Coltishall has been home to many different aircraft. The English Electric Lightnings came in 1963 – the Historic Aircraft Flight" (now known as the Battle of

Britain Memorial Flight) took place. The last Lightnings left in 1974 and were replaced by the Anglo-French SEPECAT Jaguar. The first Jaguar squadron No. 54 arrived at Coltishall in 1974.

The Pink Panther Jaguars took part in the 1991 Gulf War Operation GRANBY and Operation Warden, and no lives or aircraft were lost.

Coltishall was also home to the Search and Rescue (SAR) helicopters of 202 Squadron and latterly 22 Squadron (Wessex). But soon the SAR operations were moved to R.A.F. Wattisham in Suffolk.

The U.K.'s Ministry of Defence announced that the station at Coltishall would close by December 2006, when No.6 Squadron transferred to R.A.F. Coningsby. The final flight from Coltishall was by Jaguar X2 112 piloted by Jim Luke on 3rd April 2006.

The Jaguar was formally named the "Spirit of Coltishall" and was moved to the grounds of Norfolk County Council at County Hall, Norwich.

Now part of the station has become Her Majesty's Prison Bure and there is Badersfield, Badersfield is a modern village consisting of houses that were married quarters of the airmen, and named after the legendary Douglas Bader.

# THE TUCK FAMILY

Allan Tuck was a postmaster in Fakenham and Wells and moved to Stiffkey to live. Allan loved cricket and did a lot of work to prepare the cricket square on the new playing field at Stiffkey.

Allan had two sons, Adrian and Evan. Both went to Fakenham Grammer School and played cricket to a high standard. Adrian was captain of cricket and opened the bowling. He also bowled for Stiffkey. Evan was a year younger and after Adrian left school, Evan spearheaded the attack. Fakenham Grammer School had a very good side captained by wicket-keeper/batsman Frank Tyce.

I remember when I was playing for the school U15 XI and we played Paston Grammer School in North Walsham. I was sitting in front of Evan on the way back on the bus and I asked "How did you get on?" "We won", said Evan. "Did you get many wickets?" I asked. "7-31 replied Evan. It must have been about forty years later when I met Evan at Cromer, when he was playing for Norfolk over 50's, I said "Do you remember getting 7-31 against Paston?" He remembered.

Adrian had moved away and did some very important work. Allan and his wife Murial moved to Sheringham in the 1990's and Allan passed away there.

Evan played for Cromer for many years and eventually was selected to play for Norfolk. He has a son Kieran who was a good cricketer, a batsman. Evan played regularly for Norfolk over 50's. He still opened the bowling but obviously he was not as hostile as when he was younger.

Evan's son Kieran Tuck, played for Norfolk in 1994-95 and has now retired from active participation. He is however, the Norfolk County Cricket Development Officer.

# DENNIS PAYNE

## HIS FAMILY

Dennis' father Tom Payne was a chauffeur for Col. Granville Duff of Heydon Hall, near Corpusty. Col. Duff was part of the Duff, Vermont, Morgan – the car people in Norwich.

Col. Duff was also head of Norwich Union and for one year Mayor of Norwich.

When Tom Payne was fourteen and working in the garage at Heydon Hall, Col. Duff fell and in jured his arm. Tom took swift action and drove the colonel to the old Norfolk and Norwich Hospital.

The colonel recovered and becuase he thought Tom's driving was so good, he made him his chauffeur. He drove the Armstrong Siddeley, 20 HP with a pre-select gearbox. Tom drove the colonel all over Europe and America – he had a driving licence for seven countries.

Tom was waiting for the colonel in a hotel in Chicago when he met Al Capone, Tom thought he was "A nice chap".

Col. Duff died in 1936 – he left Tom enough money to allow him to build a shop in New Road, North Walsham, to sell confectionary, tobacco and hot peanuts.

Tom and his wife May ran the shop until 1963 when they retired and moved into a bungalow. Toms son Dennis, took over the shop in 1997. ?Dennis and his wife had two daughters who took over the shop and turned it into a flower shop called "Poppies".

## HIS MUSIC

On June 6th 1944 Dennis cycled to Roughton Village Hall with his accordion – he played for ladies who were knitting balaclavas for the troops. Dennis was paid 7/6d.

Dennis thought he would try the double base and played with Tubby Hayes and Ronnie Scott's jazz bands, in London and in the Norwich Cellar Jazz Club.

Dennis had been playing keyboards, meanwhile and in about 2001 formed the Den-Barrie Duo with Barrie Eke. He also plays base guitar  with the Old Codgers and the Lumiere Rouge Jazz Band, and the New Orleans Mick Murphy Four.

Dennis is 84 and still going strong!

# PLAYHOUSES AND PLAYERS

Until 1757 the Playhouse was at the White Swan Pub (Opposite St Peter Mancroft Church). It had benches and two stage boxes.

In1757-1758 Thomas Ivory built the "New Theatre":-

The curtain went up at 6.00pm.

Prices:-        Boxes 2/6
Upper boxes 1/6
Pit 2/-
Gallery 1/-
Upper Gallery 6d

There was a rival playhouse at the Red Lion in St. Stephens Street.

The New Theatre attracted some of the biggest stars including Sarah Suddons.

In 1777-1778 the following works were staged:- "Lionel and Clarissa", "The Beggars Opera", "Polly", "Henry IV", "Cymbeline", "King Leah and his Three Daughters" and "Macbeth".

Eliza O,Neill appeared in 1818.

The present Theatre Royal opened in 1826 with "The School for Scandal".

Prices were :-     Dress circle 4/-

Upper Circle 3/-

Pit 2/-

Gallery 1/-

Paganini, with his violin, was at the theatre in July 1831 and Liszt came in 1840. Barnum brought Tom Thumb and Blondin was at the theatre in 1869.

In 1885 the era of Musical Comedy started. Fred Morgan was in charge of the theatre. He was a remarkable man, the sone of George Morgan, the organist at Ely Cathedral.

Well remembered we the Robertson comedies, under the direction of Tom Robertson Junior.

In June 1891, Wilson Barrett appeared for a week in a round of plays, finishi8ng on the Saturday with "Hamlet".

Bed Greet was a famous name who came to the theatre. He came first in 1890 in "Village Priest". Greet brought H.B. Irving to Norwich at Christmas 1894. Irving appeared in "Masks and Faces".

Edward Compton came to Norwich. He was the father of Fay Compton and Compton Mackenzie, the novelist.

At Christmas 1905, when Murray King and Clark produced "Bluebell in Fairyland", the girl who took the lead role at the age of about 16, and made a notable impression was Gladys Cooper.

H.A. Lytton was often in Norwich with D'Oyly Carte Opera. He was there in 1926, playing and singing beautifully, in "Lilac Time".

In 1913 the building was enlarged. By 1926 the theatre was a much more comfortable place. In 1926 there was a production of Bernard Shaw's "Saint Joan" and in 1927 Eden Philpotts' "Farmers Wife."

From 1926 the theatre struggled to survive. In June 1934 the theatre burnt down. A big crowd gathered to watch its demise.

Jack Gladwin, who had managed the theatre for some time, said he would get it rebuilt in time for a pantomime. This was overambitious but it was done in just over a year, at a cost of £75,000.

The Lord Mayor opened the rebuilt theatre in September 1935, and joined the audience for a production of "White Horse Inn". In 1936 Sybil Thorndyke and her husband Lewis Casson appeared in "Six Men of Dorset".

The theatre was facing stiff competition from the cinemas that were opening. In 1939 Jack Gladwin had a serious operation and decided to stand down. He agreed to lease the theatre Prince Littler for 21 years. Littler struggled and with the Second World War looming, Jack Gladwin, having recovered from his operation, took charge again.

Many buildings in the City Centre were destroyed by bombs, but the Theatre Royal remained intact. During the War years, when theatres in London were closed, Gladwin managed to get such stars as Donald Wolfit and Evelyn Laye to come to Norwich.

In the 1950's the theatre struggled to make a profit. Jack Gladwin retired in 1956 at the age of 81. His friends L. Kemp and J. Will Collins took on the theatre. Collins was the father of Joan and Jackie Collins.

They could not make a go of it so Gladwin sold out to the Essoldo Cinema Chain, in late 1956, Essoldo showed films until in 1962 a live show was put on – "Billy Liar" starring Albert Finney. It ran to very poor attendances.

In the mid 1960's, many cinemas were being transformed into Bingo halls.

The Hippodrome closed in 1959 and was demolished in 1966.

There was much wrangling about making the Theatre Royal a "Civic Theatre". In October 1967 the West End musical "Robert and Elizabeth" was staged and lost over £3,000.

Lawrence Hill took over the management of the theatre and he brought the Osipor Balalaika Orchestra over from Russia. The receipts topped £20,000 over the fortnight.

In May 1968, the Bolshoi Ballet appeared and sold over 20,000 seats in a fortnight. This was followed byu the play "Not Now Darling" starring Donald Sindon and Bernard Cribbins. It sold 9,000 seats. By June the theatre was making a profit.

Renovations to the theatre took place in 1970. The theatre opened again in the December with the "Nutcracker", by the London Festival Ballet.

Hill retired in 1871 due to ill health. Richard Condon took over in 1972 at the age of 34. In the summer of 1974 he staged Ray Cooney's "There Goes the Bride". In 1976 he staged "Pyjama Tops" which contained some nudity. In 1979, Fiona Richmond, the nude model, appeared in "Yes We Have No Pyjamas".

Dick Condon Management Ltd. took over the "end of the pier" seaside shows at Cromer and Gt. Yarmouth. By 1989 the theatre needed much renovation and there were terrible conflicts as to where the money could be found.

Work started in 1991 and was completed in November 1992. The Syd Lawrence Orchestra was the first act to appear – a week later the Royal Shakespeare Company performed "A Comedy of Errors". Next Lionel Blair opened in the Christmas Pantomime "Cinderella".

Peter Wilson took over the running of the theatre in February 1992.

For    10 years up until 2005/2006 the Theatre Royal made a profit. Total turnover was over £7 million and the profit was £115,000.

Since 1926 the theatre has been renowned for its pantomimes. In the 1970's and 80's Yvonne Marsh often played principal boy – traditionally a part played by a woman with good legs.

In 2008 the Theatre Royal celebrated its 250th Anniversary.

# BAYFIELD HALL
# (NEAR LETHERINGSETT)

Sir Alfred Jodrell (Bart.) 1847-1929, owned Bayfield Hall and wanted to help the people of Glandford who were tithed to his 2,000 acre estate. He inherited the estate at the age of 35 and made it clear:- "I intend to leave the estate in better condition than when I inherited it."

He planted many trees and carved out a lake, which is fed by the River Glaven. He stocked the lake with fish and this practice has continued to modern times.

Sir Alfred was the only surviving son of Major E. Jodrell and a forebear of Professor Jodrell of Jodrell Bank Telescope fame.

He practically rebuilt the village of Glandford. His farm workers could then live in comfortable cottages while many land workers lived in squalid hovels.

He would send a covered wagon every school day to take the children of Glandford to Holt school, a distance of 4 miles.

When there wasn't enough work on the farm Jodrell would send his workers to build stone walls around the estate. The wall was not completed because of the First World War.

He had Glandford Church renovated – the church is high on a hill to prevent it from being flooded by the Glaven River. The church has some beautiful stained glass windows made by Kempe and Bryans.

At the end of a pew in Glandford Church is a carved copy of Landseer's "The Shepherd's Chief Mourner" In this case the dog was Nimble —the pet of Adela Monkton Jodrell, Alfred's mother, to whom he was devoted.

King George V, while staying at Sandringham, visited Bayfield Hall for a few days pheasant shooting. Jodrell wasn't very interested so he left the management of the day to Colonel Kennedy, of Wiveton Hall. However, George V wanted to shake hands with his host so Jodrell reluctantly was called forward.

Jodrell had many hobbies. He collected teapots of all shapes and sizes, and china birds. He acquired a large collection of shells, for which he built a museum in Glandford, which is now open to the public, from Easter Saturday until the end of October.

At the age of 50, Jodrell married Lady Jane Grimston, the daughter of the 2$^{nd}$ Earl Verulam. They had no children. Jodrell became ill and was cared for by James Pointer, one of his gardeners. After his death he was buried in Letheringsett Churchyard, under a modest stone. He bequeathed Bayfield Hall to his Godson, Roger Coke.

Roger Coke was the youngest brother of the 5$^{th}$ Earl of Leicester. He lived in Holkham Hall from 1929 – 1947. From 1947 he lived in Bayfield Hall, until 1960, when he died. His niece was the mother of Robin Combe, to whom he left the hall in 1960.

Robin Combe is a Liberal Democrat and was a member of North Norfolk District Council, He has now retired and left Bayfield Hall to his son, Roger Combe.

# MORE MOORES

Peter Moore's grandparents were Herbet Charles and Rosette Moore of Riverside Rod, Kirby Bedom.

Peter's dad, William, married Maud but was killed in 1944 in Holland. Peter's grandfather on his mother's side was a drayman and his horse always knew the way home, when perhaps his owner didn't.

Peter William Moore went to Nelson Street Infants School in Norwich. He then moved to West Earlham and went to Larkman Lane Junior School. He progressed to the City of Norwich School (CNS). He left at the age of 17 and got a job as a Draughtsman at Structural Steelworks, from there he went to Barnes and Pye at Tuckswood. They designed the Tower of Westlegate, the first tower in Norwich.

At about 20 Peter got a job in the County Planning Office in Thorpe Road. He went on to join the Norwich Planning Department at City Hall where he met Ann, who was to become his wife. They were married in 1973 and in 1974 Peter moved to a job at the North Norfolk District Council in Cromer.

Peter and Ann bought a house in North Walsham and in 1993 Peter retired at the age of 50, when he started his own planning Consultancy business. He was elected to the Town Council in North Walsham and in 2004/05 was the Mayor of

North Walsham. From 2012 – May 2013 Peter was Chairman of the North Norfolk District Council.

Peter enjoyed his sport. At Junior school he took a hat-trick the sportsmaster gave him 6d.

As an adult Peter played cricket for British Rail Social Club, at Slowbottom Park. One week they played against Cawston who had a "swing" bowler. Peter thought "I'll try that". He borrowed John Snow's book on how to "swing" the ball at cricket. In the next match he took 6 wickets for 2 runs and later 7 wickets for 3 runs.

Peter played tennis at Cromer, and also Badminton. He was granted the "Lordship of the Manor of Felmingham".

Peter and Ann have three children, Susanna, Elizabeth and Peter Junior, and five grandchildren.

# MY PARENTS

My Dad's family lived in Stiffkey for generations. My Mum came from Blakeney. My grandmother on my mother's side was left a widow in 1917, when my grandad Tom Palmer was killed in the First World War. My grandmother had four children and one on the way. Times were very hard and I think my grandmother tried to earn a few pennies by sewing and knitting.

The children didn't have many clothes to wear and of course they were handed down from the eldest to the youngest.

Mum grew up and went into service with a lady at Ashwicken, near King's Lynn. I think Dad worked on a farm, but he loved roaming the marshes.

My parents got married when Dad was 30 and Mum was 21. Mum moved into the house at Stiffkey and looked after my other granddad, Robert, for 13 years until he passed away.

Mum had a daughter Monica, in 1945, but she only lived eight hours. I think Mum had almost given up when she got pregnant with me and I was born on 22nd June 1949, in the maternity wing at the old Norfolk and Norwich Hospital, Mum was 40.

The first thing that Dad said when he saw me was "He needs a bloody haircut."

Before I was born Mum used to run a small Fish and Chip shop. She made most of her money from the troops who were at the Army Camp at Stiffkey. She managed to save some to buy her cottage when she left Dad.

She only had one bit of trouble. A soldier was chatting her up. Dad had been out with his "12 bore" shotgun and arrived home on his bike. He heard the commotion and pointed the gun at the soldier. Knowing Dad he probably told the soldier to F... off. Whether the gun was loade3d I don't know, but then neither did the soldier, and he made a swift exit.

As I grew up Mum and I were doing some shopping in Wells. Mum wore corsets and she went into a shop run by Mrs Cave. I didn't go in because it would have been embarrassing. When she came out Mum told me what had been said. It must have been when Mr Heath became Prime Minister. Mum had to wait her turn and while she was waiting Mrs Cave said to her customer – "Now we'll get them back where they belong." I thought slavery was dead.

That is why I will never vote Conservative.

*If you will forgive the indulgence – this chapter is about me*

# A STIFFKEY BOY

Stiffkey is a small village on the North Norfolk coast between Wells-next-the-Sea and Blakeney. It is famous for its cockles, "Stewkey Blues" and the Rev. Harold Davidson, the "Prostitute's Padre".

When I was born in Stiffkey , in 1949, there was a Primary school, near the church and three shops: the Post Office and stores run by Mr & Mrs Tony Wright, a grocers and drapers run by Mrs Codman, and another small shop run by Mr & Mrs Derek Smith.

There were also three public houses – the "Red Lion" which closed down for a while and is now open again, in an expanded form, the "Townsend Arms", which is now the Lamp Shop, and the "Victoria", which was at the end of Bridge Street.

Cricket was played on the Home Hills, which were very steep and hardly suitable. Then a local farmer, Mr Harrison, donated a field in Hollow Lane, for use as a playing field. We spent many hours picking up stones from the field. The grass seed was sown and we had a children's corner with swings, a seesaw and a sandpit. A football pitch was marked out and after due preparation a cricket square was created.

I spent many hours practising football and cricket on the field and one of the silliest things I did was long-jumping in the sandpit. Instead of planning to land in the middle of the sand I jumped from the edge and landed on the far edge, which was concrete. I sprained my ankle very badly!

There were three men who roamed the marshes regularly. One, Mr Ardine Jarvis, did his gathering for a living, although I'm not sure how much he earned. The other two did it as a hobby. One was Mr Joe Jordan, who was to be the "warden" and received a medal for saving people who got into difficulties on the marshes. The other one was Mr Bob Baker, my Dad.

Dad was a bit naughty but in many ways quite clever. He was a bit of a poacher and we had pheasant for Sunday lunch on many occasions. He said he never had a problem with a gamekeeper or similar. The only time he was frightened was when he stood on a sleeping horse and it reared up at him.

When it came to fishing Dad was quite clever. He could spot a flatfish, a dab, in the sand, under water. He made what he called a "butt fork". He took a long round piece of wood and straightened out two large barbed hooks and tied them to the end very tightly. Then he would wander round the creeks spotting the dabs in the sand and stabbing them.

Dad had an accident with his "Butt fork" one day. It was leaning up against the shed and protruded above the roof a little bit. Dad was on the shed roof and missed his footing. He landed on the "butt fork" and the hooks, complete with barbs, went into his bottom. We called a neighbour, John Buck, who sawed the "butt fork" down to a manageable length and then John took Dad down to Wells Hospital. We were fortunate to have Dr Hicks as our G.P., who was a surgeon and he cut the hooks out. Dad had a bit of trouble sitting down for a few days!

Another method a catching fish was "laying lines". He would take a long piece of rope and tie, say, 50 small hooks on nylon string to the rope. Then 50 lugworms would be dug, this was hard work on wet sand. The worms would be attached to the hooks at low tide. The tide would come in and after it had receded he would go back to see how many fish had been caught. Sometimes he wouldn't get any at all and sometimes he would get as many as 20, one never knew.

Then there were cockles, winkles and in the summer, probably August, samphire. Dad did not normally get mussels. Mussels were gathered when they were young and put in "mussel lays" by the fishermen They were then left to grow and were harvested when they were a good size. It was bad form to take mussels away from someone else's "lay".

We were also never short of wood for a good fire. Dad used to gather wood that had washed up, especially after a big tide, and bring it home on an old bicycle, the large pieces were then sawn down to the right size for the fireplace and the best pieces were chopped for kindling.

Sometimes it had to dry out and we had a shed at the bottom of the garden where Dad had a small stove. When he had been busy sawing or chopping you could sometimes find him asleep on a bench in the shed.

Dad enjoyed a smoke. He rolled his own but I don't know how many he smoked because he usually had a cigarette in his mouth, but half the time it wasn't lit.

Of course we ate some of the goods we got from the marshes, but any surplus was sold. We used to put a board up on the side of the road to advertise our wares. We didn't make much but it all helped.

There used to be quite a lot of cockles at Stiffkey and Morston was a good place for winkles. When I got old enough to help I used to go down to the marshes with Dad. He would only take me to places that were safe, he didn't take me to places where I might be cut off by the tide. If you went cockling together and got quite a lot on a Wednesday, then we had a regular customer, Mr Eke, on Fakenham market every Thursday. Mr Eke would sell them on the market or on his round the next day.

The cockles were sold "live" in Imperial measures, usually by the "quarter peck". A "peck" was two gallons, so a quarter peck was half a gallon, or four pints. This was too much for some people, so we would sell them   two or three pints.

Of course, some people didn't know how to cook them, so we told them. It is quite simple really but may sound a bit gruesome. They were heated and when the shells opened they were ready – the cockles weren't able to hold the shells closed.

I suppose you could say that Dad was a sportsman being a fisherman and a shooter with his "12 bore". Mum was very serious but I was her "golden boy" being the only child. I was more interested in sports where a ball or balls were involved, football, cricket and billiards.

Mark Jarvis, who was a very good footballer, was captain of Stiffkey Minors until he was too old to play – he went on to play for Holt. I took over from Mark as the powers that be liked the captain to live in Stiffkey. I think Colin Firmage was secretary and treasurer and then I took over those duties as well as the captaincy.

Throughout we had a very public minded figure guiding us – Stanley Sutton. Stanley was on the Parish Council, the Playing Field Committee and Chairman of Stiffkey Minors Football Club. He was also a qualified football referee and refereed many of our home games. Stanley still lives in Stiffkey but he is getting on a bit now.

When I was seventeen or eighteen Mum left Dad – she thought I would be old enough to understand. We moved to a small cottage which Mum was able to buy. I had a Mini by then and used to drive to Morston to get the school bus. I stayed on at school until I was nineteen. In the summer holidays from school I thought I would earn a bit of cash by cockling as they were quite plentiful at that time.

Depending on the tide I would gather the cockles in the morning and go round selling them in the afternoon, or vice versa. I sold most of them in Holt – I thought the Wells people would be getting their own, being on the coast. On one occasion I was wheeling the sack of cockles off the marsh on a bike, when Dick Bagnell-Oakley and two others approached, Dick asked me a couple of questions and filmed the cockles as I showed them a handful. A few days later a school friend said "I saw you on T.V. last night". I had had my thirty seconds of fame! When I was nineteen I left Stiffkey to attend the North Western Polytechnic in London.

I returned to my Mum's cottage in Stiffkey in 1988, at the age of 39. Mum was in a retirement home in Fakenham. I tried a bit of painting and decorating but there was a lot of competition and Autumn is not the time to start. I had some capital from the sale of my flat in London, and as I loved sports, I thought I would open a Sports Shop. I settled in Cromer and opened in March 1989 – the official opening happening with David Gower, the Leicestershire and England cricketer. I'm afraid the shop was not a success.

Since leaving Stiffkey I lived for five years in Sheringham, and for the last eleven years in North Walsham.